THE LONG MARCH HOME
An American Soldier's Life as a Nazi Slave Laborer

Published by Hellgate Press
(An imprint of L&R Publishing, LLC)
PO Box 3531
Ashland, OR 97520
email: sales@hellgatepress.com

Editor: Harley B. Patrick
Book design: Michael Campbell
Cover design: Stephanie Kromash Baum

Cataloging In Publication Data is available from the publisher upon request.
ISBN: 978-1-55571-891-6

THE
LONG
MARCH
HOME

*An American Soldier's Life
as a Nazi Slave Laborer*

ROBERT R. MAX

DEDICATED TO THE MEMORY OF MY
WIFE AND PARTNER OF 67 YEARS,
SHIRLEY BILLER MAX.
THIS STORY WOULD NOT HAVE
COME TO LIFE WITHOUT HER LOVE,
GUIDANCE, AND INSPIRATION.

CONTENTS

LOOKING BACK

I TRIED ON THE ARMY JACKET—the one I wore when I was discharged from the military in December 1945, the one bedecked with the battle ribbons and medals. It no longer fit. Sixty-nine years had gone by.

I thought of that day…

I stood there frozen—frozen by fear, frozen by the bitter, biting cold air. Shrapnel from exploding American or British artillery shells landed on the ground around me. I tried to squeeze into the German sergeant's bunker. "*Nein*," he grunted, his rifle pointing at my chest. I wanted to run, but the presence of guards and other German soldiers in adjoining bunkers made escape impossible.

"What are you going to do with me?"

In surprisingly good English, he replied with seeming indifference, "We have to kill you."

PREFACE

FOR 53 YEARS, I gave little thought to the possibility of writing about my experiences as an American soldier in World War II and the events that followed, but questions from my grandsons helped me to recognize that the story of my survival in combat was very different from anything I was aware of in print or film.

"Were you in the war, Poppy?" nine-year-old Emerson asked. "Where did you sleep? What did you eat?"

Xander followed with, "Did you have a gun? Did you ever shoot it? Did you ever kill anyone?"

I had spent the most brutal months of World War II as an unregistered slave laborer for the German Army, the very enemy I had enlisted to fight. Unlike other American prisoners of war, I had been a victim of Nazi atrocities. Although I was an American soldier, my war experience more closely mirrored those of Jewish concentration camp detainees who were sent on "death marches" towards the end of the war.

Had I been registered as a POW, I might have been afforded the protections granted under the Geneva Conventions, shelter, heat, food, and bed and bathroom facilities. These conditions were nothing elaborate, but would have been considerably better than exposure day and night to sub-zero temperatures, starvation, "sleeping" outside on the snow and ice-covered ground, beatings, and the threat of being shot for failure to perform assigned work. The proposition was simple: You worked (repairing bombed railroads) or you died. And many did die.

Elie Wiesel (left) with Shirley and Robert Max in 1988.

Inspired by Elie Wiesel during a weekend in 1988 that my wife Shirley and I spent with this Nobel laureate, profound author, and chronicler of the Holocaust; and motivated by Xander and Emerson, I felt an increasing obligation to break my silence and add my name to the growing list of Holocaust survivors who were finally speaking out, many for the first time. The world must know and must remember that six million Jews were murdered by Adolf Hitler and Nazi Germany. And so I started to tell my story. By coincidence, I learned about the Holocaust Council of Greater MetroWest NJ, a division of the Jewish Federation of Greater MetroWest NJ. Council director Barbara Wind invited me to share my experiences with students in public and private schools and universities. These opportunities allowed me to reach a vital and sensitive audience as I released my memories of the war and the Holocaust to generations well into the future, part of the mission to ensure that the world would "never forget."

Now, years later, I have spoken to thousands of young people in public schools in New Jersey, where Holocaust education is mandated, and in other states as well. These students have become witnesses, carrying the messages of the outcomes of war, genocide, and survival to future generations. In the closing pages of this book, I include excerpts from some of these young people's letters, in which they commit themselves to the mission—to remember and to speak to others years in the future so that there will always be voices carrying the memories; voices of reason that will stand as deterrence to any future atrocities.

My memoir reveals the life-and-death struggles encountered in battle, including my capture during the Battle of the Bulge; and the harsh physical treatment, starvation, and almost intolerable physical and emotional pain I experienced as a Nazi slave laborer. The story culminates in a desperate escape. I am one of the few American soldiers known to have successfully escaped their German captors and survived.

I also chronicle my recovery at military hospitals in Europe and America. It took me almost a full year to recover from the physical trauma of captivity. The healing of my psychological wounds would take much longer.

When the first World War II soldiers returned home, they were greeted as if they were celebrities. My own homecoming was no different, and I share my memories of a nation and its people as they reached out to their returning soldiers with gratitude in response to our service during a most critical period in American history.

Wartime experiences generated a transformation in my character, and my future goals were largely reshaped during the sleepless hours of my hospitalization. I felt that life had become more precious. Survival stirred in me a compulsion to serve, to do things for others beyond my immediate sphere of influence and contact.

Years earlier, I had been inspired by Rudyard Kipling's poem "If," which includes the lines:

> *If you can fill the unforgiving minute*
> *With sixty seconds' worth of distance run,*
> *Yours is the Earth and everything that's in it,*
> *And—which is more—you'll be a Man, my son!*

At 93 years of age, I am one of a dwindling number of surviving World War II veterans. Sharing my unique wartime experiences with a wider audience has become one of my personal goals and the inspiration for this book.

The events, conversations, and memories
portrayed in The Long March Home are
based on my recollections, many dating back
70 years and more. I've tried to present them
with clarity, and through the best of my
ability and memory, as they occurred.

CHAPTER 1:
A CALL
TO DUTY

2

Sign Up to Serve –
We Were at War:
Fort Dix, New Jersey

HOW CAN I describe the appeal of military life in 1943? Our country was in a war we hadn't started but couldn't avoid. While entering the fight was not attractive to all, it did hold a certain appeal for many of us. It was popular to be part of the war. Some were driven by patriotism, others by conscience.

For me, maybe it was a bit of both. I often read *The New York Times*, specifically searching for news reports of Adolf Hitler's war on the Jews. Such reports, though, seemed to be buried among the later pages of the *Times*, and that concerned me.

While I believed the Ochs-Sulzberger family, the owners and publishers of the newspaper, were Jews, I was to learn that some had converted to Episcopalianism. Why were these stories about the Jews as targets of the Nazis not front page news? Was there an anti-Semitic sentiment?

Reading the limited reports and the discovery of the merciless killings probably influenced my judgment in signing on to the war effort. When I enlisted, my hope was that I would wind up in the European Theater of Operations. Like many Jewish young men eager to serve, I wanted to confront the Nazis and help stop their war against the Jews.

In the predominantly Jewish fraternity house at Ohio University where I was living with 20 other students, we often had late-night bull sessions, with the conversation often turning to the war. With American news sources reporting daily on the campaign in Europe came additional stories of Jews being massacred by the Nazis. One by one, my friends and I seemed to be subliminally signaling to one another that our obligations lay outside the university's walls. It was a new sensation for me.

The bull sessions in my Phi Epsilon Phi fraternity house made their mark. As a group of young men at similar states in our lives, we were moved to sign up. We did what so many others did. At age 20, I left a comfortable campus life and enlisted. As it would turn out, Reserve Officers Training Corps (ROTC) at the university would give few clues to what military life was like.

Once the determination to sign up became real, we faced the reality that we might never again assemble as fraternity brothers—and that we had a good-sized bank account. With so many members now heading off to war, we knew we would have to close down the fraternity home for an extended period of time. With the future uncertain, it didn't make sense to leave a full bank account untouched during our absence, so we decided to spend it all.

During the closing months of the school year in the spring of 1943, Phi Epsilon Pi became the gourmet center of Athens, Ohio. New York's finest steaks and chops could hardly have been better. It became socially significant on campus to receive an invitation to dinner at Phi Ep.

(An interesting note: Those of us who returned after the war and attempted to restart the fraternity discovered that we had no treasury, no money. My fraternity brother Dave Friedman of Cleveland suggested that we incorporate and sell non-voting stock. Who bought the stock? Our parents. We were on our way. A year later, I was elected president of the Alpha Rho chapter of Phi Epsilon Pi fraternity as well as the president of my university's Hillel Foundation. These were my first steps on a path that would ultimately lead to many leadership roles in the Jewish community and beyond.)

You're In the Army Now

NEW JERSEY'S FORT DIX was one of many Army induction centers throughout the country. It was a staging area where we were to be conditioned to what was for most of us a very different lifestyle. We had to be weaned from civilian self-determination to a kind of regimentation that had to be shaped gradually.

First impressions sometimes last a lifetime. Sighting the barracks that would be my home for weeks or months ahead, I was struck by its stark appearance: a long grey building with three steps leading up to its entrance. The landscape was no better—building after building. They all looked alike. Thank goodness for the numbers posted outside each barracks.

Bedrooms and privacy gave way to cots and public latrines. Alarm clocks and late night radio news were replaced with shrill—and at times, piercing—sounds of reveille and taps. The "Bugle Call Rag" became just the bugle call.

Marching drills were the order of the day. Discipline was instilled in this early stage of a new Army career. And there were other duties: KP, or kitchen patrol, for example. If the Army lived on its stomach, it was surely the potato that was the core of its sustenance. KP duty called me for kitchen and dining room setup, cleanup, and of course, peeling potatoes; endlessly peeling potatoes.

Our barracks were our homes; policing them our duty. Order and cleanliness were a matter of policy. And so we were measured on the neatness of our footlockers and the tidiness of our beds and "living" areas. It all required work, and we were expected to perform diligently. We were also judged on the firmness of our bed sheets. Officers inspected the barracks and dropped coins on the sheets to see if the coins would bounce. I was diligent and produced tight bed sheets; coins bounced. Those whose sheets didn't make the coins bounce received demerits. There were penalties for the demerits, which were posted outside each barracks.

Music and the Military: Another Way to Serve?

SEVERAL DAYS AFTER my arrival at Fort Dix, I was summoned to the company office. I was told I was being granted a weekend pass and that I was to return with my saxophone and clarinet. How did they know that I played? This was long before computers could reveal intimate details of our lives. Somehow, though, my pre-war experience with dance bands in New Jersey and Ohio had gotten into my records.

I remember that on my 10th birthday, I awoke to find a clarinet at the foot of my bed—an unexpected gift from my parents. I must have shown some early interest in music.

I took lessons, later adding alto saxophone, and was ready to pursue an experience with big bands in the 1930s. I not only played, but studied the popular big bands of that period and learned to recognize the members of those bands, the sidemen.

During my freshman year at New York University, I planned my classroom schedule to run from Monday through Thursday, leaving Friday free to spend the day at the Paramount and Adams theaters in Newark. Friday was special in my world—it was opening day at the theaters for some of the country's leading orchestras.

As a beginning young musician, I was entranced with the music of the big bands of that period. I remember one Friday when two of America's most popular bands came to the theater stages in the same week. They just happened to be led by the two greatest clarinet players at that time (if not ever), Benny Goodman and Artie Shaw. I was delirious with joy. I had been playing clarinet and alto saxophone with local bands for several years. Momma packed me a sandwich and soda and sent me off by bus to Newark for one of the most thrilling days of my life.

Playing music in an Army band was far from my pre-enlistment expectations. I was entering the military, prepared to (temporarily) give up everything to do what military people do: to prepare for combat and ultimately face an enemy—nothing heroic, simply an act of responsibility. That was what I told my parents, and while my mother was worried, my father supported my decision.

Fort Dix had assembled an outstanding group of musicians, sidemen who performed with the top big bands of Tommy Dorsey, Les Brown, Harry James, Benny Goodman, and others. Jack Leonard, a handsome, smooth-voiced singer who preceded Frank Sinatra as vocalist with the Tommy Dorsey orchestra, led the Fort Dix Swing Band. Jack wanted me to join the band, and evidently that was enough for the officers in charge to send me on my way to South Orange, New Jersey, to retrieve my sax and clarinet.

What a shock at my first rehearsal! I was intimidated—I was sitting next to the best musicians of the time. Most could compose and orchestrate, and some had attended institutes like Juilliard in New York City. I wasn't in their class, but managed to survive. While scared, I was thrilled to play alongside professionals, America's best, and those I had hoped to emulate in my pre-war years.

Home on leave in South Orange, New Jersey, 1944.

With the band assignment, Army life could have been an excursion to easy living. Over the next month, my days were filled with more leisure than I had known in a long time. Morning schedules were of my own making for practice, and I enjoyed afternoon rehearsals and some evening radio broadcasts. No chores, no potato peeling. A wonderful way to wage war. Or was it?

One day, my name appeared on a list; I was to be shipped out for basic training, preparation for combat. At the request of Jack Leonard, the order was set aside; I was to remain with the band, and ironically, probably sit out a large part of the war. Whether it was the search for adventure, the desire to serve as others were doing, or a matter of conscience, I don't know, but I asked not to be excused from those shipping orders. "No, Jack," I said, with some reluctance, but knowing I would have experienced a feeling of guilt or abandonment if I hadn't. We were at war, and I just didn't feel comfortable watching some of my buddies shipping out. And what would I say years later when someone asked, "Were you in the war?"

I told Jack I expected to be back with the band someday. "Kid," he said, "you leave now and you're not ever coming back." Prophetic. The decision made, destiny took hold. I was headed for basic training and real Army life.

Tough Training Makes Good Soldiers: Final Preparations

FOLLOWING A CIRCUITOUS train ride, I landed at Fort McClellan, Alabama. Some called it "the hell hole of the South." As military camps go, it had all the facilities one might expect—barracks, mess hall, drill staging sites, field obstacle courses, and a marksmanship shooting range. What it also had was a cadre of hardened Army veterans, many of whom had served in combat units. They weren't about to let a bunch of smart-aleck college kids escape the hardships they had endured in service.

Basic training was rigorous—deliberately stretched-out marching drills, obstacle courses, physical and mental torment. When one bivouac and forced march over challenging, mountainous Bain Gap wasn't enough to break us, they tried another. They marched us, in full combat uniforms and burdened with backpacks and rifles, in temperatures hovering around 100 degrees. After one march under a blazing sun, they stood us in an open field. After some time, I became faint and wobbled, but refused to fall. I barely remember the march back to the barracks, but I sustained myself until I fell onto my bed, barely conscious. We survived—all but one of us, someone I had known as an English professor at Ohio University, where I had transferred from NYU before entering the service.

He was older than all of us, in his forties, and not in good physical condition. Unable to complete the exercises for the obstacle course, he ultimately received a medical discharge. I was sorry to see him go. For me, though, my mind and body were strengthened by the ordeal. It would later save my life.

Notice the pompadour. That's the way
some of us wore our hair, even in the Army.

Unlike the rest of the week, Sundays were special—a reminder of sleeping late and asking Mom to rustle up some pancakes or eggs. At the mess hall, I ordered what I wanted, and the cook made it to my specifications. I followed a routine: two eggs up with whole wheat toast one week, pancakes with sausage the next. Breakfast was not only pleasant, but also a time to "schmooze," share photos from home, and gossip about the cadre, our trainers. It made returning to drills on Monday more difficult, but it was well worth it. It was hard to believe that this was the Army, and we were preparing for war.

In contrast to this one pleasant memory of Fort McClellan, I also recall the frustration of seeing bronzed, shirtless German prisoners of war laughing, smoking, and enjoying the privileges of shopping at the Post Exchange while they ridiculed the forced, heat-exhausting marches we endured in heavy military clothes and equipment at blazing temperatures. Oh, how I wanted to break ranks, dash over, and bounce my rifle right off their skulls.

Now, years later, I'm reminded of the irony in all of this. I don't know what happened to all those German captives. But I do know that going through what they ridiculed—what seemed like abusive training at the time—probably helped save my life while I was in captivity and under the control of their comrades.

A New Wrinkle in Army Preparedness

GOING FROM FORT McCLELLAN to Auburn, Alabama, while no great distance, was a transformation in lifestyle. Alabama Polytechnic Institute, later known as Auburn University, was home to an Army Specialized Training Program (ASTP). I was assigned as an engineering student to the unit based there.

The US Army needed engineers and language specialists, and reached into its ranks for trainees. Military vehicles had to be maintained, pontoon bridges built. Translators of foreign language documents and conversation were essential parts of military intelligence.

Typical of the US Army selections process, leadership often chose GIs with no civilian experience, so that they might be trained to function the Army way. I had no training or education in engineering; no collegiate math, science, or engineering. But an Army entrance test revealed that I had a reasonably high IQ, so I was qualified.

Dormitories replaced barracks and tents. While military discipline was enforced and marching and fitness drills were routine, study and exams became part of our lives. We spent long, grueling hours each week in actual classroom work plus preparation time each night and on weekends.

But dormitory life had its moments—events that gave us relief from the routines of military life. We let loose on Saturday nights, when two close friends from New York City and I planned and produced our own off-off-off Broadway shows. We posed as musical impresarios, calling ourselves MKM Productions (Herb Maneloveg, Charlie Kwartler, and Bob Max). We staged productions featuring the greatest music of our time (all recorded on commercial records we got from home) and attracted an overflow crowd of our student soldiers in my stuffed dormitory room. We listened, some sang, and we all enjoyed pretzels and soda (no beer allowed). The feature attraction on opening night was America's Greatest Black Musicians. The entertainment: the recorded music of Duke Ellington, Jimmy Lunceford, Earl "Fatha" Hines, Count Basie, Ella Fitzgerald, and many others. The shows were big hits and provided a release from the stressful dual life of soldier and student.

With this kind of interlude at Auburn University, for these short periods, we were able to embrace the lives we left behind and nurture great memories and dreams of what life would again be like when war ended. For a short time, we were living in a dream world. How could we have known what lay ahead?

There's a War On

WHILE OUR ALLIED troops advanced aggressively across France, infantry casualties mounted, and combat-ready forces were needed overseas. ASTP became a casualty. The program had to be sacrificed to a greater need. Herb, Charlie, and I talked a lot about the impending change in our lives. Herb, philosophical, accepted fate; Charlie, ranting, was just plain not happy. I accepted the reality that there was a war on. Ground combat, we knew, was dangerous and dirty. Most of us wanted to avoid it.

When it became apparent that ASTP would be terminated, many of us at Auburn applied first to air cadet training in Montgomery, Alabama, and later to Officer Candidate School at Fort Benning, Georgia. The exams we were required to take were reasonable, and I think we all did well on them—but perhaps not so much on the intimidating interview we had to go through.

At the Officer Candidate School, I remember being ushered into an austere darkened room. To my right at a long table was more "brass" than I had ever seen in one setting: Army officers, and not a welcoming look among them.

This was the interview that would help determine if I had the essential qualities for leadership. Intimidating? I was a "young" 21, not accustomed to being grilled, particularly by such an imposing group of questioners. The questions were reasonable, as I recall, but I never did learn the results of the interview.

Our efforts at both the Air Cadet School and Army Officer Candidate School were thwarted by a more critical need. The Army simply had to reinforce the depleted ground troops in Western Europe.

I've often wondered if I would have made a good officer, one who could draw the respect and confidence of subordinates. Up to that point I had never held a leadership role. I had additional strikes against me: I was probably younger than any soldier I might have led, and I looked it. I was short: 5'4", well-built and athletic, but still short. The average male height at the time was about 5'8" or 5'9". I was certainly not an imposing figure.

Training for Combat: Top Priority

CAMP ATTERBURY in Indiana was my next stop. I would finally link up with a unit preparing for combat, the 106th Infantry Division. I had to learn to be a combat infantryman. But as I soon discovered, I had a dual role to play: one with a rifle, the other with a jeep.

Training took on a greater sense of urgency. Through lectures and manuals, we were introduced to simulated battle conditions, and came face to face with the consequences of war: soldiers killed one another, and the better prepared we were, the greater the chances of survival and ultimate victory. I learned early on that a rifle would become my best friend in combat and that caring for it might save my life. It was a US M-1 Garand .30 caliber rifle. I learned to take it apart and reassemble it in the dark, and I became comfortable with it on the firing range. Maintenance was important. But another kind of maintenance would soon occupy my time and training.

We were often assigned to roles in which we had no experience. I ended up in the motor pool in a combat training unit of the 106th Infantry Division, where I was expected to help maintain jeeps and trucks.

The only thing mechanical I knew was that the automobile engine had spark plugs and a carburetor. And the only reason I knew that was because my father had inherited my grandfather's 1925 maroon Cadillac (built, incidentally, like a tank). Many Sundays, on a family outing, we would drive up South Orange Avenue in South Orange, New Jersey. It was hilly, and partway up, the engine would stall. Not to worry. My father grabbed a wrench, lifted the engine hood and tapped on the carburetor, then got into the car and drove off. Residue from the gasoline had clogged the carburetor. The spark plug, I discovered, created the spark to ignite the gasoline.

> *I observed the procedure, and there I was, an "expert" on the internal combustion engine. I knew little more than that, but with some training, it made me eligible to become a member of the motor pool, responsible for auto maintenance. I did my job the Army way, the way the Army preferred.*

Responsibilities in the motor pool called for more than vehicle maintenance. I chauffeured officers to meetings and other assignments, and that turned out to be a relief from the drills required for combat readiness. I enjoyed driving and getting to know some of the officers, hearing stories about their families and their civilian lives. Discussion often turned to their kids, sports, vacations, and the hope for the war's end and their return to their families.

Training in preparation for ground combat included handling and firing automatic weapons in addition to the M-1 rifle. I earned a marksmanship medal. While I could handle the M-1 rifle well, I never felt comfortable with a machine gun or an automatic rifle.

We were well aware of our destiny. We were being trained to reinforce ground troops in the European theater and would ship out when ordered to do so. There were no surprises — trepidation among some of the troops, anticipation among others. But how do you develop a mindset for battle? I wasn't sure I was emotionally ready for the hazards of combat.

Driving a jeep at Camp Atterbury, Indiana, September 1944.

During breaks in training, we talked a lot and tried to anticipate what combat might be like. Some of the younger guys were charged with excitement and anticipation, harboring in their innocence visions of performing heroically against an enemy that had defeated most of Europe. I remember the comment of one of these gung-ho soldiers: "Gonna get those heinies." I liked his spirit and told him so.

Others were less comfortable with the realization that we were headed for danger. I knew my own life and the lives of others would be on the line. It was the unknown, and for some—particularly the older ones—the fear that they might not be coming back that held sway.

CHAPTER 2:
INTO A DIFFERENT WORLD

rd the LCI, the realization became greater that
ded for some kind of encounter. Putting on hel-
ing gas masks, rifles, and cartridges made the
al. Nevertheless, at age 21, I wasn't ready yet
th and adventure for reality and danger. Some-
my buddies managed to bring along a camera.
t know. But unpredictable Herb urged me to be
irst to storm toward shore; as the big front end
vas lowered, he planned to get historic evidence
ing the shoreline. He raced off first and took my

l as we landed ashore and assigned to different
s, Herb and I didn't see each other again—until
fter the war, I learned that he had become an
one of the largest advertising agencies in New
t that point, I was helping a television producer
ship for one of their shows, and we made con-
gain.

inisced, recalling the Normandy beach landing.
ly, I asked about the photo. What a great
o it would be. But Herb, hands extended, palms
stant look on his face, pleaded, "Don't know
appened to it."

e as we waded toward the shoreline was sub-
ess chaotic than it had been on D-Day. I could
ne what that must have been like. I had seen
pictures of the landing and the chaos, and I
what lay ahead. As we debarked from the LCI in
o our waistlines, we faced no artillery or small

The Need for Ground Forces in Europe Increases

WITH PRESSURES MOUNTING on the European front, replacements for front-line troops became imperative. Selected for overseas assignment, I landed on one of the lists, gave up the jeep I was privileged to drive for high-ranking officers during the few months I spent in Indiana, and headed for a staging area at Fort Mead, Maryland.

Scheduled to be shipped out as a ground troops replacement, and ultimately assigned to A Company, 9th Infantry Battalion of the 6th Armored Division, I later recognized that it was only then that I made the behavioral and emotional adjustment to the realities of combat—kill or be killed, an attitude more readily learned in battle than in preparation and training.

On September 18, 1944, I boarded what had been the British luxury liner *RMS Mauretania*, heading across the Atlantic. Large floating palaces like this one were "drafted" to ferry troops overseas. I had never been aboard an ocean liner, nor even seen one, and the sight of this ship was overwhelming. In earlier pre-war trans-Atlantic trips, the ship had been distinguished by its stark white color. When I stood in awe at its side, it had been repainted in battleship gray. I presumed that would make it a less identifiable target for German submarines lurking below the Atlantic Ocean.

The procession up the gangplank was slow and wearying, as we carried all our equipment on our backs. For a while I forgot that the ship's mission was to deliver us to the European continent and ultimately to battle with the enemy. I could only think that I was entering a period, brief though it was, of new adventure and the pleasure of sailing in a magnificent vessel.

Once aboard, reality struck. Thousands of us were jammed together. There were no lounge chairs; there would be no idyllic strolls around the deck. By the numbers, they started calling us to the quarters we would share with many others, more than the space would allow.

Occupying a bunk in what had once been a cocktail lounge, I could only imagine what passenger life must have been like during the ship's transatlantic cruises. My living quarters for the next five nights must have been strikingly colorful and cheerful during the ship's many sailings. But what I saw was a stripped-down, Army-type quarters with bunks fastened to the wall, one on top of another.

We had lectures during the day and were served Army mess. There was some griping aboard ship, but this was not meant to be a happy voyage. Looking at the foamy trail left by the ship, I noted how adroitly we avoided sailing in a straight line. Doing so allowed the navigators to make tracking more difficult by Nazi submarines.

Nevertheless, as we docked in Liverpool, England on September 25, 1944, we were greeted with people exhibiting newspaper headlines declaring that the *Mauretania*, with thousands of US troops aboard, had been sunk. Our living presence testified to the inaccuracy of that journalistic scoop.

Warm beer, bland food, and bea[...] as vague reminders of a final stagi[...] don't remember much more of a[...] tion about when we'd see combat[...] our thoughts. Across the English [...] that had devoured nation after nati[...] their will to resist, and that soon w[...] recall feeling restlessness and uncer[...] soon change. Crossing the English C[...] adventurous. Liberty ships and LCIs [...] try) piloted us to an uncertain destin[...] to find that fear had not yet entered n[...]

As we approached Omaha Beach o[...] of France, we had to transfer from the[...] that would deliver us close to shore. Th[...] ships were fitted with ladder nets, and [...] 30 or more pounds of combat-ready e[...] masks, etc.), we found the descent to[...] ous. I knew I had to place each foot [...] step by step, lowering myself toward[...] Channel waves lashed against the s[...] sel bobbing and bouncing, making th[...] The two ships repeatedly slammed ag[...] then parted. The timing of the jump [...] A few never made it, I was told, and t[...] as I started to descend. I didn't see [...] the ships, but later learned that durin[...] just a few months before, some soldie[...] ships into the water and were lost.

arms fire. I don't recall any confusion as we were formed into our combat units. The enemy was some distance away.

It was now September, three months after the initial D-Day landing. While we could make out the sound of distant shellfire, the only serious obstacle we found was the severely pitched trails, which made the climb difficult. We marched past the deeply imbedded German pillboxes from which the enemy had poured down artillery, batteries of rifle and machine gun fire. No wonder D-Day casualties were so high. I stopped, turned, and paused at one of the pillboxes and tried to imagine what it had been like inside. I looked at the cannon and pictured shells ejected, and endless streams directed at and striking so many of our invading troops. "Move along, soldier," I heard, as one of the group leaders urged me to catch up with my unit.

It wouldn't be long before the distant sounds would grow closer. Moving eastward, I began to understand and appreciate how the earlier bivouacs during training had prepared us for what lay ahead. Experience had made me ever more adept at putting up and striking a tent.

But the setting here was vastly different. During training at Fort McClellan in Alabama and Camp Atterbury in Indiana, we bivouacked many times. It had been good preparation for not only putting up and striking tents later in combat, but in getting accustomed to comfortable living in a different environment. Back in the States, I felt confined and insecure inside my tent. Strangely, as we approached combat and danger, I was "at home." I guess it was because the tent was the only and closest thing to shelter and protection I had. The bigger issue, though, was the reality that there was still a long, forced march ahead, and our mission was to fight, not sleep.

I recall the impressive massing of troops as we headed for combat. Our 9th battalion numbered somewhere around 500, and "A" Company about 150. Working down the chain, we became closer working units, with about 20 to 30 in each platoon and 5 to 10 per squad. I rarely got to know anyone beyond my squad or platoon.

October 1944, just two months before the Battle of the Bulge.

There were seven of us, though, who were all former college students, all about the same age, and with common interests. We called ourselves The Lucky Seven—lucky, I guess, because we had found one another. Though I am not good at remembering names, one—though not a member of The Lucky Seven—stands out: Luke Saleme, tall and skinny, a backwoods type, with little formal education. He was soft-spoken and light on conversation, but when he did speak, it was clear he knew what he was talking about, and so he became a leader. I don't remember if it was of the platoon or the squad, but we were willing to follow him, and we did.

On our way to the front, we encamped in a wooded area outside a small French village. The village had been plundered earlier by the Nazis, and the locals were pleased that American soldiers were now nearby. One of our squad or platoon members, from Brooklyn, New York, jovial and with a command of the French language, approached one family. I don't know what he said, but they hit it off. To show their appreciation, they invited The Lucky Seven to a dinner in their small but comfortable home, an experience that to this day remains vivid in my memory for its excellence in food, drink, variety, and revelry.

One dish followed another, including rabbit, which I had never eaten before. With great fanfare they served us wines, cognac, and calvados that they had concealed from the Germans. We were their saviors, and they were determined to let us know. What I didn't know, though, was my limited tolerance for the combination of spirits.

Attempting to leave the small country cottage, I keeled over at the door and had to be dragged to my tent. While my tentmate Herb, a veteran party goer, threw up and dozed off, I was unable to do so. I handled the overindulgence the only way I could: walking, running, and sweating it out.

Because we were approaching a combat zone, camp security was tight. My senses, dulled by the alcohol, were incapable of alerting me to the dangers of guards with rifles and fixed bayonets. On my first inebriated tour, with no warning, one of the guards lunged. I must have staggered, and he missed. The routine repeated itself at each post. After the first circuit, guards were expecting me, and the hazard of running into a bayonet lessened.

It must have been three or four in the morning before my head stopped whirling and I was able to lie down. There would be no sleep that night, though. Soon the shrill sound of whistles filled the air and orders rang out: "We're moving out!" Tents were struck, the area policed, and with 30 pounds or more strapped to our backs, we set off on foot. Later, the realization hit me: here was the kind of forced march, testing our will, strength, and stamina, that we had endured in basic training at Fort McClellan, and yet men dropped with regularity by the side of the road. It was more taxing than many could withstand.

What was unexpected was that our Lucky Seven made the march with no dropouts. Medical science might have had an answer. My simpler solution was that fortified by wine, cognac, and calvados, we were insensitive to pain, torture, and emotional stress. We just continued, oblivious to those "minor distractions."

Treated by Army medics, the dropouts were restored to battle readiness and soon rejoined us as we marched to our first encounter with the enemy.

Entering the Battleground: First Contact with the Enemy

FROM FOOT SOLDIERING, we moved to mechanized travel as we became attached to the large 6th Armored Infantry Division. Surprisingly, I rather quickly made the transition to the half-track, a light-armor, protective open body supported and moved by tank-type tracks in the rear and wheels up front. A mobile home it wasn't, but what little comfort there was to be had, it provided.

The half-track is an anomaly. While it provides a shield against small arms fire, it is a clear target for heavy artillery. The ranking officer sat next to the driver in a completely covered cabin; the troops lined up four or five on each side facing each other in the rear of the topless vehicle. We surely were vulnerable as we were limited to easily targeted roads. Just how vulnerable, I discovered a short time into my first day in combat.

Aboard the half-track, some unusual events occurred, leaving lasting impressions. I had not seen the enemy under combat conditions. Suddenly, many emerged in disarray from wooded areas to our left. Their hands raised in surrender, rifles discarded haphazardly, some ran, others walked toward our vehicle. One of our men leaped to the mounted machine gun, firing randomly at the targets as they moved toward us. We shouted to cease fire, but it took a while for our trigger-happy gunner to stop firing. When he finally did, other American forces came along to take the surrendering Germans as prisoners.

This was my first battlefield interaction with the enemy—the first time I saw men shot. Because we continued in our half-track, I wasn't sure what happened to them and didn't know how to react. I didn't see it as a triumph. But now I had seen my first Nazi warriors, who looked like anything but warriors—and certainly not members of a superior race, as Adolf Hitler had anointed them.

As the half-track gathered speed, my thoughts remained back on that battlefield, on those men willing to concede defeat. Or was their willingness to concede *opportunism*?

Some of those Germans might have known (through repatriated German POWs) that life in an American POW camp would be good. I had been an eyewitness to the treatment of German prisoners sent to American military posts. During basic training at Fort McClellan, I saw them behind fenced-in areas—relaxed, tanned from the southern sun, in good and sometimes high spirits. They enjoyed the privilege of buying cigarettes, candy, and more at the Post Exchange. For them, life was good, and they laughed as our trainers put us through our paces.

Could these surrendering German soldiers have known? Tired of warfare, fearful of injury or death, or simply cowards, I can only suppose that is why some of them might have been willing to trade the battlefield for the security of an American prisoner of war camp.

During those early hours of day one, enemy shells passed over our vehicle. Members of our squad—some of them veterans of battle in North Africa—plunged to the floor of the vehicle. Their memories triggered an immediate reaction to seek cover. I had not yet seen an exploding shell and the devastation it left, so I didn't react at all. I would soon learn that failure to react quickly could be deadly.

Evidence came later that same day. Moving toward an intersection in an area the Germans had abandoned, we were suddenly overwhelmed by mortar and heavier artillery shells. The lesson of vulnerability quickly seized me. Roads and anything on them are easily targeted, so we moved the vehicles off the road to a nearby open field. German artillery struck nearby and passed overhead with a "whish-y-whine" sound. Those we could hear were not the ones to fear; they passed beyond us. The shells that struck gave no warning.

We dashed from the half-tracks to spots that provided some cover. For me it was beneath the rear end of the vehicle. I recall signaling to other squad members who had scurried for cover under the front end. I still didn't get it; this was hide-and-seek, still a game for me, despite the wounded I saw being carried off on stretchers. I had yet to become truly sensitive to danger and the imminence of destruction and death. The next morning that would all change.

"The enemy strikes at dawn." It was an adage that had had little meaning to me, until...

The haze had begun to lift, and what was dark started to fade into view almost minute-by-minute. I could see our tanks spaced neatly across a field, poised for battle. And then we heard that terrifying sound that made men scramble for any form of protection they could find. It was the early morning "incoming mail."

Shell after shell exploded around us. The Germans hadn't zeroed in yet; there was still time. But I had no refuge. All that training and all those warnings hadn't been enough to convince me that under enemy fire, a soldier's best friend is his foxhole. Foolishly, I hadn't dug one. While others threw themselves into the excavations they had carved for themselves the night before, I had nowhere to go.

Suddenly my body was jolted as a shell fragment split the barrel of the rifle I was holding and tore it from my hands. For the next few minutes I felt helpless and further endangered. My right hand ached; the rifle barrel was inoperable. Someone came from somewhere and gave me a replacement—maybe it was from one of our men, wounded or killed by enemy shelling. I don't know, but I was grateful for the gun, momentarily stunned, and saddened by the loss of a comrade.

Finally came the revelation: *This is a serious business, and you could be killed in a split second.* Many during that attack were. I had sought cover beneath the rear end of a tank, a terrible choice. It soon moved and I had no protection. But fortune had been with me that day, and I would live never to repeat the mistake of ignoring warnings born of experience.

The Battle of Han-sur-Nied

DURING MY FIRST two days in combat, while attempting to evade enemy shellfire, I remember the troops talking about a place called Han-sur-Nied. The only thing any of us knew about it was that it was a town on the river Nied, and that it and we were in the Lorraine region of France. The lieutenant leading our platoon had been briefed, and some of us talked with him about our mission: to get across that river. He didn't pull any punches, warning us that getting across the bridge would be dangerous.

German troops had occupied the area. As they retreated under relentless attacks by our forces, they managed to aim their artillery at the spot where we would be expected to cross the river. The scuttlebutt was that the mission was too dangerous, the odds insurmountable. Most were not too eager to try; I was ambivalent. As members of A Company, 9th Infantry Battalion, 6th Armored Division, we probably would be at the point of the attack. Officers leading our unit would have to make the decision.

We fought as ordered and started across the bridge. Shells landed nearby. Was I scared? Sure. I was beginning to recognize that shelling was common in ground warfare. You never really get used to it. Any of those particles of metal could penetrate your skin at any moment. It's best not to think about it. But under heavy enemy artillery, we succeeded in crossing the river on foot and began to advance in pursuit of the enemy.

This came to be known as the Battle of Han-sur-Nied, and it was a brilliant victory for General George Patton's Third Army and the 6th Armored Division. But there were many casualties that day, and I remember reading sometime after the war that historians had called Nied "the river of blood."

So this was combat. And though I didn't realize it at the time, it brought many lessons about life, some that would shape my thinking and performance in the future. I later came to view the battle as a kind of model for warfare—a combination of strategic planning and courageous execution—that would serve me well as I planned business ventures later—though, of course, under very different conditions.

I also learned about discipline, about listening and loyalty, about seeking goals and objectives, and later, about cruelty and punishment and the inequities of life.

Sitting in the half-track—as we moved forward while not under attack—produced at times an indefinable nothing; just empty, unfocused thoughts. Sorrow and empathy set in when I witnessed American soldiers shot, killed, or wounded; and often, I paused and wondered why them and not me.

Fear and vulnerability held a constant presence, as artillery landed nearby or gunfire from rifles and machine guns stalked us. Seeing American soldiers struck, killed, or wounded—some in great pain—and the call "Medic!" streaming from our voices left me with some bad memories.

On the battlefield, I was gripped by the realization that a shell fragment or bullet could pierce my skin without warning. I believe others thought the same. I don't recall ever talking about it, though. It was something we just got used to.

During the second day of combat, we abandoned our half-track. In it, we were sitting ducks for German artillery. We were instead ordered to proceed on foot, reducing our risk of detection and becoming less susceptible to enemy shelling.

As foot soldiers, we encountered predominantly rifle and other small arms fire, though we were still the targets of enemy artillery. Soldiers in front of me and behind were struck. I paused; I hadn't seen this before. A man lay on the ground... dead, never again to witness, to be part of the experiences of life. And his family... what about them? Their lives would never be the same. Here was another reminder of the brutality and unforgiving reality of war.

I sometimes wondered how many among us questioned "Why me?" Some remained stateside; others served in non-combat roles, while we served under enemy fire, not by choice, but by chance.

I learned to live with that, thank goodness, because it too was part of adjusting to the realities and the inequities of life. There are times when you just get to be lucky; other times when you have to take what life serves you. And we were getting our share of it.

The Army Cared for Its Own

IN COMBAT WE were fed well. Some complained about C-rations and D-rations. But I loved them. Festive Thanksgiving and Christmas meals were served even though we were in a combat zone in hostile territory. I well remember Thanksgiving dinner in 1944. There were no table settings. I was on my own. With my tray full of turkey, dressing, and cranberries, I went hustling up a hill to my foxhole. Enemy shells landed nearby or passed overhead, forcing me to use juggling skills to keep my mess kit from bouncing out of my hands. Strange, but I can't imagine the emotional stability that allowed me to down a meal with "bombs bursting in air." As the shelling lessened, I closed my eyes and tried to imagine what family, friends, and others were doing back home. I looked at the turkey in my kit and remembered that in my family, nobody liked turkey—too dry—so on Thanksgiving we ate goose and duck.

Unaware of the dangers of tobacco, we lit up and we smoked, sometimes excessively. It filled some of the emptiness, substituted for the relaxing after-dinner smoke back home. Each puff released some of the stress imposed by battle conditions. Packages from home were delivered no matter where we were. Cookies, cake, candies, and salami were welcome treats, supplementing the battlefield diet dominated by baked beans and Spam.

What really lifted our spirits was the mail that followed us all the way to the battle zones. I waited anxiously for my name to be called. Was it a letter from Momma, sister Ruthie? Mail call, early many mornings, found us still reading as we massed into combat units.

I remember the lines in a letter from Momma: "Poppa is out patrolling the neighborhood tonight, and he's wearing his helmet." I chuckled, and paused for a moment, stunned by the realization that I was fighting the war the way the Army wanted me to and Poppa was fighting it the way his country wanted him to. But, in South Orange, New Jersey? We learned later that German submarines had lurked off the coast of my home state.

My parents' contributions to the war effort were typical of so many Americans' urge to serve. The Rosie the Riveter character—representing women taking on "men's work" as the men marched off to war—became famous. Momma sewed garments needed by the military. Signs in public places encouraged people to buy war bonds, and people did. Butter, beef, gasoline, and silk stockings were rationed, automobile factories converted production from cars to tanks and ships—and nobody complained.

This was an America we had never seen, and one that many believe we will never see again. I was so proud as I read Momma's letters, as impressed with their contributions as I knew they were with mine.

The weather became bitterly cold as December approached, a month that would prove pivotal in the war. We were well clothed. The US took good care of its soldiers. It received much in return.

Danger Lurked Everywhere

ASSIGNED TO A surveillance team, three others and I were ordered to reconnoiter strategic enemy territory, determine the size and battle preparedness of the German troops, and report back to company field commanders, all under cover of darkness. "What are we looking for?" one of the team asked.

"We'll know it when we see it," I assured him.

It became completely dark. With our sharp, body-piercing fixed bayonets attached to our rifle barrels, we trudged off through the snow and toward whatever fate held in store. What we found was a small unit of Germans, platoon size of about 20 or 30.

They are well armed and seemingly battle-ready. Carefully, unseen, we head back to our lines, emotions high for fear of running into a battery of enemy guns. Suddenly, a bayonet emerges from the heavy brush, and behind it a tall man, menacing, prepares to ram it into my torso. Inches away, he stops, pulls it back, and shouts "Bobby!"

> *Stunned, reflexes taking over, I withdraw the rifle I'd instinctively raised to fire on an apparent assassin.*
> *His voice is familiar; he's clearly not a German. As he emerges from the brush, I see a ghost... but no, he's real. It's my long-time friend Mel Kirzon, who moments ago was a split second away from a rifle blast, while I was inches away from a sword of death.*

"What are you doing here?"

Mel and I had been friends at Ohio University in 1942. As easterners—he from New York City and I from nearby New Jersey—we had many interests in common. Our friendship had carried us into the Army, and chance had us assigned to the same combat forces, though in different battle units.

When he contracted an illness that couldn't be treated in a combat area, he was taken to a field hospital for treatment. He had apparently recovered and returned to his unit, and he and I, each on similar missions, met up in this most unpredictable way.

"Mel," I said after stabilizing my emotions, "I can't believe it's you! You've recovered, I see, but did you have to scare and almost bayonet me to death?"

"Bobby," he replied, "in the dark and under these conditions, I thought I saw the enemy."

A strange conversation ensued. Others in our unit stood by, bewildered by it all.

But we didn't have time for much discussion. Data gathered, our mission fulfilled, we headed back to staff headquarters and delivered our report.

Later, tucked away in my sleeping bag and reliving the experience, I kept repeating "Can't believe it—could've been killed by my long-time friend Mel." That night I revisited many of the disparate scenes... on campus, at military training bases in the US, on battlefields in France. The memory has remained, while others have subsided or been forgotten.

CHAPTER 3:
THE LONGEST WINTER

The Battle of the Bulge: Climactic Battle of World War II in Europe

BRITISH AND AMERICAN forces, after breaking out of St. Lo in the western part of France, raced across the country. However, Allied intelligence, while alert to German preparations, could not have predicted what was about to happen.

On December 16, 1944, the German Army struck with unbridled power, massing some of its forces and creating a bulge that broke through Allied lines and threw our combat units into disarray. We had been in battle for three months. Deep snow drifts covered the ground, making movement more difficult for us. My unit followed the lead of the 4th Armored Division, and swung 90 degrees north to provide support for the beleaguered American 101st Airborne Division, which had been defending against the Germans' drive toward the Belgian town of Bastogne. I learned later that we were pitted against a cadre of former Hitler Youth, well equipped with tanks and guns, and charged by Nazi rhetoric. They had already achieved a record of bravery and brutality.

Following the initial attack by the Germans, the unit I had originally trained with in Indiana, the 106th Infantry Division, was reported to have lost 75% of its forces—killed, wounded or missing on the first day of this climactic battle of World War II. The scuttlebutt among our troops was that the 106th was "green," not ready for combat.

Those numbers startled me. Some of those men were my buddies; we had shared photos and talked about our families. I wondered who among them were casualties. I speculated about what my odds of survival might have been if I had remained with the 106th instead of becoming a replacement assigned to the 6th Armored Division.

Serving in the motor pool while training with the 106th, I had chauffeured several officers. We talked a lot during some of the drives—about their families, mostly about the kids; about sports and personal interests. I had really gotten to know some of these men, and I could see their faces. I remembered some of their names and could only hope that they would someday return to the families we had talked about.

On January 4, 1945, after three days on the line, I was ordered to the rear for some badly needed food and rest. Then I heard a call for volunteers to return to the front. We had lost radio contact and could not identify battle lines. Commanders were limited in their ability to develop strategy without knowing positions of Allied and enemy forces. I commandeered a jeep and signaled to five others, who piled on. We headed for where we thought the troops were, unaware that the US Third Army had withdrawn to regroup for a major counterattack.

The roads were covered with snow. A gray mist filled the air, limiting our vision. While believing that we must be nearing American lines, we were stunned when instead we were suddenly confronted with an 88-millimeter cannon mounted on a German tank-like vehicle looming perhaps ten yards before us. We had crossed into enemy territory. Instinctively, I slammed on the brakes. The jeep spun and landed in a ditch, inoperable. We dashed to the left, across the road, to escape the direct line with the 88. Had anyone inside the tank chosen to fire, we'd have been dead. For a long time afterward, I wondered why they hadn't.

As machine guns started to clatter, a small gray shack to our left appeared to be our only refuge. We made a mad dash. One soldier didn't make it; he was shot in the back as we raced toward the shelter. The sound of automatic weapons filled the air, bullets whizzing by.

When the other five of us reached the shack, we could see across the road where all that firing was coming from. With the little protection it offered, this shack became our fortress, the road separating us from the German forces, our moat.

One of our team had had the presence of mind to quickly unbolt the jeep's machine gun and carry it with us as we raced across the road. I moved toward the .30-caliber gun when the man behind it toppled, a victim of a Nazi bullet. The machine gun was mounted at what had been a large bay window, fully exposed to enemy fire. With no time to assess the odds of being hit by positioning myself in that window, I acted spontaneously. I took no special precautions; perhaps battlefield readiness kicked in, making me react aggressively to danger.

Gripping and squeezing the trigger, I fired countless rounds at whatever I saw move, unaware that I was depleting what little ammunition we had left. I fired to kill, and probably did kill many. One of our group decided to break in the direction of what he thought might be our Allied lines. He didn't get more than 25 yards before he was cut down by enemy fire.

I discovered later that day that the remaining four of us had traded rifle and machine gun fire with an estimated 100 Germans. As twilight descended, two of our group, firing from the only other front window, were wounded and needed medical attention. The two of us remaining dwindled what little firepower we had left in the expectation that the Germans would assume that they had eliminated this small band of Americans and finally bypass us.

The machine gun sputtered; I had spent the last bullets we had. A shiver ran through my body.

Discovering a trap door in the floor of the shack, I recognized that there must be a cellar. Perhaps it would offer us temporary shelter and time to plan a strategy for survival. We lowered the wounded and crawled below. We waited, lying still and quiet except for the groans of the injured. What seemed like an eternity passed.

Our plan was to wait for darkness to fall, then emerge and attempt to infiltrate enemy lines by picking our way through a mesh of trees and German soldiers. We would have to determine if the wounded could move with or without our help—a difficult decision, one we never got to make.

Perhaps an hour after descending, I lifted the trapdoor, moving it to the side. I glanced upward and caught sight of a vision that has imbedded itself in my memory: a ring of black automatic weapons, barrels pointed straight down at my face. Behind each, trigger finger poised, was a white-cloaked German soldier, camouflaged to blend with the snow outside. It was dark, late in the wintery afternoon. My apprehension and then fear intensified as I stared first at the gun barrels and then at the poised trigger fingers and faces of the enemy.

Wartime memory is experienced in different ways. Some events are forgotten, some of those intentionally so. Some are vague memories; and some, like this one, remain clear, distinct, embedded in your mind. (As I write these pages, I stop and close my eyes; the scene of that encounter is vivid. I shudder, pause, and go on writing.)

I heard a voice say in English, "How many of you are down there?" I responded, and we were told to climb out of the cellar. But how did they know we were there? The wounded had been unable to keep silent, and it was the sounds of their suffering that alerted the Germans to our presence there.

We lifted out the wounded and crawled up ourselves, and then everyone except for me was taken away. I never saw any of them again, and I don't know what happened to the wounded.

The unit commander chose me to verify that there were no booby traps in the shack. Alone and isolated, I felt more vulnerable; in fact, scared. Then, at rifle point, I was nudged through the door and across the road by a German sergeant, the commander of the group. Suddenly shellfire began pouring in from Allied artillery—support we had called for earlier in the day. While the Germans descended into their bunkers, I was forced to remain above, terrified by this sudden bombardment.

The Struggle to Remain Alive

THE SKY WAS ablaze; in a nearby field, flames rose from an American tank ignited earlier by German artillery. I watched helplessly. As I stood there, rifles pointed at me while shrapnel and fragments from artillery shells landed all around me. The Allied artillery filled the air, the ground, and the trees surrounding me. Ironically, I was now among its targets. How I craved shelter!

Stretching to see as far down the road as I could, I realized why the battle had gone on hour after hour, and why the enemy just kept emerging, no matter how many rounds we fired. Foxhole after foxhole lined the road. Nazi helmets and machine guns rimmed the edges of a long row of neatly dug protective bunkers.

How I would have liked to climb down into one of those bunkers. "*Nein!*" the sergeant barked as I attempted to do so. I was now his prisoner, and as a prisoner, I was denied the protection my captors reserved for themselves.

And so, with ideas of escape abandoned, I turned to an alternative—conversation. The German sergeant understood enough English for us to exchange views. Our priorities, though, were quite different. I don't know how I maintained the emotional stability to carry on a discussion with an enemy committed to killing me. As I think back about the incident, I can only surmise that there are times and conditions when instinct takes over and when we are able to reach beyond ourselves.

With shells still exploding and fragments landing nearby, the realization that I was perhaps minutes from being dead suddenly gripped me. Aware of an order issued by the German high command that no Allied prisoners were to be taken alive, I asked with some trepidation, "What are you going to do with me?"

The response was unhesitating: "We have to kill you."

I don't recall much that immediately followed other than my almost uncontrollable urge to bolt down the road and perhaps back to Allied lines. I had been a sprinter in school. All the training and skills honed by competition could possibly save my life. The road, though, was as brilliantly lit by the nearby burning Allied tank as Times Square on New Year's Eve. But what I saw quickly convinced me that I'd be riddled with bullets right out of the starting block: bunker after bunker, a machine gun mounted on each.

I was pinned to the spot, standing above my captor.

Then, a surprise. The sergeant, relatively secure in his foxhole, decided to share some thoughts with his captive American soldier. Shouting over the rumbling and blasting of artillery, he said he expected to go to New York when the war ended. "I will take my family so they will see the big city of yours," he told me.

I wanted to tell him he didn't have a chance. But suddenly he reached into his pocket. I assumed he was retrieving the pistol that I knew as a non-commissioned officer he would likely be carrying, to do what he had told me just minutes before he would have to do: kill me.

Instead, he pulled out a photograph of his wife, son, and daughter. His flashlight wavered, but I could make out the image of a decidedly handsome family.

He glanced up at me from his foxhole, and then gazed at the photo. Perhaps he saw in me a young American, not much older than his son and perhaps not much different in appearance: blue eyes, blond to light-brown hair.

We were on a battlefield where soldiers were fighting and killing, but he seemed to defy the profile of a Nazi warrior.

As we talked, the mood changed. There was a softening in his tone; with his command of English, there was none of the harshness blended with guttural sounds of his native tongue.

And yet, unlike many of the German soldiers we had captured earlier, the sergeant was still passionately committed to victory and could not understand what we Americans were even doing there.

"This is not your war," he said, almost pleadingly.

"But you made it our war," I replied with surprising logic, considering the circumstances.

So we were combatants, enemies pledged to defeating and killing one another, and he had been among those targeted when I had fired from the shack. But at the same time, he knew our team had been greatly outnumbered—the six Americans against his hundred or more troops—and managed to survive. Even though I was the enemy, I believe he saw me as a soldier serving his country with valor, and he viewed me with respect.

But I wasn't completely sure. When he said, "You killed some of our men, but you fought well. For you, the war is over," I listened intently; for a moment, I expected him to point his rifle at me and fire.

Instead, he said, "I'm going to send you to a prisoner of war camp."

Stunned, I pondered how to interpret his remark. Here was a good and loyal German soldier who was defying orders from the higher command. Could I trust what I thought I heard? With Allied artillery shells still exploding in the trees around us, I had little choice, and I even began to feel a sense of security. While he would not go so far as to offer me shelter in his bunker, I sensed he had decided that I didn't deserve to die and that he was, in fact, committed to saving my life. Our conversation even suggested to me that this soldier just might be a humanitarian.

When I heard him declare his plan to remove me from the battlefield to a POW camp, I even started to feel a bit of comfort. During my basic training at Fort McClellan, where many German captives were confined, I had seen the decent treatment they received, and I expected the same at a German POW camp. I'd be housed in a barracks, I thought, with my own bed, heat from a wood- or coal-burning stove, sufficient food to keep me alive, toilets (instead of the slit trenches we often dug ourselves, covering them after use), and facilities for maintaining hygiene—even for cleaning and shaving.

And, of course, in a POW camp, there would be no heavy artillery or bullets. I would no longer be a target.

I saw my capture by this particular soldier as perhaps a kind of miracle. He had expressed admiration for the battle I and my fellow soldiers had waged against him and his soldiers through a long, beleaguering day, and this might have been his way of rewarding the valor he recognized in me.

It was a strange parting as I left the German sergeant. I had some lingering doubt as two assigned guards ushered me forward, a rifle digging into my back, as we set off for the POW camp.

Uncertainty – and Reality

I EXPERIENCED A range of emotions—fear of the unknown, what might lie ahead, abandonment by the German soldier who saved my life, and loneliness—while it was just me and two German soldiers plodding through deep snow and the heavily treed area of the Ardennes forest.

But as the hours passed, it became more and more apparent that a traditional POW camp was not to be my destiny. A German officer had stopped us, and I believe he countered the sergeant's order. We pivoted and moved in a different direction.

Prodded by a rifle barrel pressing against my back and traveling along a narrow road, I was stunned sometime later to see a mass of unfamiliar uniforms—dozens of captured soldiers, many apparently from other countries. I later learned that they were from Eastern European nations—mostly the Soviet Union—and had been captured during Germany's invasion in 1941. To avoid the harshness of impending slave labor, many had actually volunteered to join the German Army, and fought in Normandy against the American and British invaders. Most, however, suffered and starved in labor squads.

We had become unwitting comrades, indiscriminately formed into work units, and—as I discovered later—we would be forced to repair railroads bombed by Allied aircraft. Confused and slightly dazed, I moved wherever the rifle butt of my guard pushed me.

My memories of the events that followed are vague; I suspect I blocked out some of them. I do know that I recognized that we were under the control of well-armed German guards and that following their orders was the only way to stay alive.

Two guards yanked the heavy winter coat from my body and pulled off the gloves protecting my hands. Resistance did no good. One guard in front held my shoulders while the other pulled the coat. I wondered how I would take the frigid air, the snow and ice.

Orders rang out. Pointing with their rifles, guards motioned for us to get up and get going—our first forced march. After about an hour of trudging through snow, I had a sinking feeling in the pit of my stomach. Where would I end up? What were they going to do with me? As dusk and then darkness set in, we were ordered to lie down in a single line on the side of the road; to sleep, if we could. It was the forerunner of months of frigid, sleepless nights on frozen and sometimes snow-covered ground. And for the first time, I felt what it was like to be nameless; I hadn't even been assigned a number. I was submerged in a mass of humanity whose members were indistinguishable from one another.

While I had had optimistic expectations of what it meant to be a POW, I soon discovered that what I had anticipated bore no resemblance to life as a Nazi slave laborer. We were not registered as prisoners of war; these Nazis had no use for the rules of the Geneva Conventions regarding POWs.

The code under which we labored was simple: work or perish. We were expendable.

For the next several months, stripped of my identity, I was herded with other captured men, working and struggling to advance on the frozen terrain, often through snow so deep that the energy required to trudge through it induced more fatigue than the work we were forced to do. Our task: to rebuild the railroads destroyed by our own Allied bombs. Conditions grew continually worse. Though we were not under enemy fire, there were times I would have traded the torture of slave labor for the dangers of combat.

Men too weak to work or who simply refused were beaten. Every day, men died from exposure, sickness, or a rifle blast. I felt the urge to attack a German guard as I saw him shoot and kill a prisoner unable to lift himself from a resting position. A member of our unit told me the soldier's name; it was easy to remember: Eisenhauer.

To keep us alive, they fed us a crust of bread each day—heavy, almost indigestible brown bread—and occasionally hot water they called broth, with a small piece of potato and little flavor. Force-marched for miles at a time, at one point we passed through a labor camp in Prum, Germany where we were fed six crackers, one inch in diameter. That was our single meal for the full day. At the camp in Gerolstein, we got a little variety: a canteen cup of flour and water and a sixth of a loaf of brown bread. We remained in each camp for less than a day.

Adding to the anguish of the malnutrition we suffered, we frequently witnessed our captors gorging themselves on meat and other plentiful food. They devoured their meals with glee, well aware of the emotional and physical torment they were inflicting on us.

My mind and body ached. At first, it was just a gnawing in the pit of my stomach and a craving for food; and then, an emotional reaction—a realization that if conditions didn't change, I could eventually starve to death. As the days wore on, I started to feel weaker; my feet felt heavier with each step. The unending labor and marching continued to deplete my energy and strength. I knew that if I dropped out, as I had seen others do, I'd either be shot or left to die. Those unable to work were of no value. The German guards seemed incapable of compassion, and I expected none. I used every bit of energy I had, and when I felt that running low, I was able to call on my reserves. I had the advantage of youth and an athletic body.

For some time, I was consumed by the sight of the faces and the crumpled bodies of the dead. Memories of those images frequently led to despair, and I would again have to summon an emotional reserve.

Whenever conditions plunged and I feared the imminence of death, I was sustained by two possibilities: that the Allies would soon win the war or that I would find a way to escape. I wanted to talk about it with my fellow prisoners, but we were barred from conversation. I was lonely, frustrated, and frightened.

I knew that Hitler and his Nazis had an additional wartime agenda besides military conquest: to rid the world of Jews. In defiance of my captors, hidden beneath my shirt on the same chain that held my dog tags— which identified me as a Jew—I wore a star of David and a tiny mezuzah, a

Jewish amulet containing prayers and a reminder of God's protection and the importance of faith.

It was standard procedure to wear our dog tags beneath our shirts. If I had been a registered POW, I likely would have been interrogated and required to expose them; I would have done so without reservation. Whether it was fate or luck, I was never asked to show my tags. Perhaps to the Nazis overseeing my captivity, religion was unimportant; they were interested only in work, not in ideology.

Young and defiant, I refused to allow the Nazis to strip me of my identity as a Jew. I wore the Star of David and miniature mezuzah next to my dog tags through combat and captivity.

Work or Die

OUR TASKS CONTINUED to be the repair of German railroad tracks bombed by Allied aircraft. A prime target of American and British forces, the railroad system was essential to moving supplies to combat troops. After forced marches, we arrived at sites covered by craters that we had to fill and jumbled masses of steel that we had to replace with tracks. Moving those tracks sometimes required strength beyond our ability, and so beatings with rifle butts or barrel staves across the back were delivered often and with force, reminding us that we had to work—or die.

Even under these conditions, we did manage a victory. Some smart guys were among us; forbidden to talk, we laborers did manage to communicate. With no intention of fixing the railroad, we had to disguise our efforts toward doing so. After we dug out the rubble, with continual prompting from German rifles, we would get the replacement tracks to the bed, ostensibly to embed and attach them and insert the steel ties. Glancing to the left or to the right, I would watch the others and follow whatever moves they were making.

I remember glances and smiles conveying satisfaction that we had successfully achieved our objective, sabotaging the Germans' plans. The guards conducted inspections, but their knowledge of railroads was limited. They did not detect the subtle misalignment that would derail any supply train traveling over these "repaired" tracks. Our success, even under these adverse conditions, sustained our emotions for a while.

What we could not avoid without risking our lives was transporting the heavy railroad tracks on our bony shoulders, sometimes from one town to another. It hurt. It hurt a great deal. But I simply could not allow it to stop me. If it had, I probably would have been shot or left to die. With the cold air around me and the frozen turf beneath me, I developed frostbite on both my hands and feet, producing painful sensations. As a youth, living a sheltered existence in pre-war years, I went home when it got too cold. Now there was no home, no one to turn to for aid. The pain, particularly in my fingertips, was at times almost unbearable. I had no gloves, and pushing my hands into my armpits provided little relief. Thrusting my fingers into my mouth, perhaps for some warm breath, drew a rifle barrel across my back. There was no tolerance, no empathy, just hard-nosed German soldiers doing their jobs, as we were expected to do ours. To avoid detection by Allied planes, we marched mostly at night when the temperature hovered near zero degrees.

The Air Force and flying held great fascination for me. While I served in the Army Specialized Training Program at Auburn, Alabama, I made a serious effort to be accepted as an air cadet trainee. In fact, when we learned that ASTP would be disbanded and we would be headed for the infantry, the effort to become pilots intensified among most of us.

*We had studied silhouettes of Luftwaffe and Allied
aircraft until we could identify every one, and further
prepared ourselves for the examination that would be
given at Maxwell Field in Alabama. We were expected
to dedicate our evenings to ASTP studies, but our study
sessions turned into mock air battles instead. We were
ready to fly, but casualties overseas were mounting, and
we found ourselves reassigned to infantry combat units.
We had believed we qualified for admission to air cadet
school and thought we were on our way to the Air Force,
but then our wings were clipped. So much for flying. I
was destined to serve my country on foot.*

During forced daylight marches, the skills I had learned
during Army Specialized Training Program allowed me to
distinguish German planes from American aircraft overhead—though identifying approaching planes as American
didn't help; the Germans had done nothing to mark us as
Allied soldiers or POWs. From the air, we were indistinguishable from the Nazi forces, and so we became targets
of Allied bombing and strafing. We would scatter and seek
shelter, but some of us were hit.

Dodging bullets was only part of the challenge. Over-
coming anxiety was just as devastating to our spirit and
desire to go on. After the attacks, the planes would loop
and head for England. Because we were under attack, we
would, on occasion, wish that the German Air Force was
still intact. They might have been able to divert the fire
from us to themselves.

As the American planes turned west, I was left with a feeling of hopelessness. We were abandoned and could look forward to nothing but cold, hunger, and back-breaking labor. Those pilots and crews were probably returning to the comforts of an officers' club, with food, drink, and a big, fat cigar.

The Luftwaffe did mount frequent, feeble efforts at twilight, flying over our locations, but it was purely symbolic. Their engines sputtered because of the inferior fuel that was all they had. They wanted to send the message that the Nazis were still able to wage war, but at this late stage in 1945, we knew otherwise.

Chances of Survival Diminish

TO REMAIN ALIVE, we had to be able to tolerate pain. Sub-zero temperatures, exposure, starvation, frequent pummeling, and mental anguish exacted a heavy toll. I remember a buddy collapsing under a load he was carrying. A few of us ran to his aid, but the guards jabbed us with their rifles. Too weak and helpless to challenge them, we stood by as they kicked the downed man and rolled him over until he lay still and died.

> *Chances for survival were greater for those who entered the war in good physical condition—a fact that I am sure played a major role in my survival. The Army did all it could to toughen our bodies and, to some degree, our minds. During basic and combat training, many of us thought such rigorous preparation may been excessive and useless. But I'm a surviving example of that kind of preparation, and the lessons I learned have stayed with me. Into my 90s, I'm as physically active as health and aging will allow, continuing a daily routine of 25 push-ups and therapeutic routines for my bad back and legs.*

Food during captivity was in less than short supply and did not vary. It scarcely existed. Mornings found us chomping on about a sixth of a loaf of dry, almost inedible hard-crusted brown bread. The pieces were thrown into a pile, and hunger drove us to fight for our meager share. Later in the day or at dusk, the guards laid out cans—similar to old Campbell's soup containers—containing some hot water, and on occasion, a piece of potato for "flavor." Unlike animals that are fed so they can work, we and our diets were largely ignored. With the lack of food came weakened bodies, malnutrition, loss of body fat and muscle, disease, and for many, death.

I remember that during a forced march, at the risk of being shot, I reached down and scooped up what appeared to be a few Brussels sprouts in a field adjoining the road. They were lying amid snow and mud. Whatever I could grab with one hand I stuffed in my mouth, mud and all. It was an unpleasant taste sensation, but it would sustain me for another day.

There were a few moments of relief, one that resulted in an atypical dinner. We were occasionally locked in unheated barns for the night; it was bitter cold, but at least we were protected against the wind and snow. On one occasion, we spotted chickens in the barn. A member of the group grabbed one, strangled it, and, as we were roused by our guards for departure, threw it in a sack he found in the barn.

The problem was the trail of blood. During the day's long march deeper into Germany, we were challenged to develop a strategy to conceal what we hoped would be our first taste of something better than bread and "broth."

We took turns carrying the sack, slipping it cautiously from one to another. It became the duty of the man behind the carrier to scuff the snow and cover the droplets of blood.

If a guard had discovered our booty, it would have led to a lot more than the loss of the evening's repast. It was easy to imagine that stealing the chicken would attract at the least a beating and possibly a bullet to the head.

But our strategy worked and opportunity beckoned. Locked in a different barn the next night, we were blessed to find some dry hay. Cooking fuel! One of the men, who had managed to conceal a cigarette lighter from the Germans, offered to ignite the fire, and we were on our way to a highly irregular feast.

But how do you divide one bony chicken among 20 or more starving men? I don't remember even plucking the bird. After burning it in the fire, with stalwart discipline we each settled for little more than a taste. I had scarcely enough to fill a space between my teeth.

Scraps here and there provided some sustenance, but not nearly enough. We deteriorated week by week. Our resistance to disease diminished, and we were prey to a variety of bacterial infections.

The contribution of mental attitude to countering physical impairment was not well understood or accepted in the 1940s. Norman Cousins, the author of *Anatomy of an Illness as Perceived by the Patient: Reflections on Healing and Regeneration* (1979), had not yet introduced his concept of humor and high spirits as aids to recovery from illness. My experience suggests, though, that imagination, vision, hope, and determination could overcome some of the most threatening conditions American servicemen lived through in World War II.

For example, I had been under the impression that thinking about food was the worst thing a starving person could do, but my experience proved the opposite. During many of my lonely hours, I drew solace by thinking of specific foods.

The loneliest times were when I was trying—usually unsuccessfully—to sleep. It was Germany's coldest winter on record, temperatures often below 5 degrees, and of course no warm clothing or blankets, and the "mattress" the hard ground frequently covered with ice and snow. So that solace came from concentrated conjuring of favored foods. The sensory perceptions were real; I could visualize, taste, and smell a plethora of foods.

I even know how many foods I did conjure up: at least 84. (Later, when I was hospitalized, a nurse brought me a small notebook, and with remarkable precision, I was able to record that imaginary "menu."). The list included apple pie, date nut bread, homemade bread, chocolate layer cake, cherry Jell-O pie (Momma's specialty), homemade fudge, stuffed peppers, lamb stew, veal chops, hash, three varieties of "pigs in the blanket" (chopped meat and rice wrapped in cabbage leaves or frankfurters or sausage baked in dough), corned beef, duck, chopped liver, meat loaf, chicken noodle soup, stuffed pork chops (only imagined, never eaten), baked macaroni, gefilte fish, fried herring, Welsh rarebit, deviled eggs, grilled cheese, baked apple, and on and on.

My imaginary feasts gave me an additional reason to resist giving up: It would all be real someday.

These are some of the foods (recorded many months
later during my hospitalization) that I dreamed
about, and that helped sustain me emotionally during
sleepless nights on snow and ice.

Among the dozens of slave laborers who toiled along
with me, one man stands out: Myron Barringer, a farmer
from Rushville, Indiana. On one occasion, he and I and
the others found ourselves housed in a barn with a single
cow. "Bob," Myron yelled, "come on over here!" An experienced hand at milking, he suggested that I lie beneath the
cow, and he positioned me in line with its udder. The pleasure I got from drinking those few heavenly spurts of milk

surpassed any I received from the finest tasting food I had ever enjoyed before—or have enjoyed since. I have never forgotten his compassion.

After the war, Myron and I exchanged greetings during the Christmas holiday season. Year after year, his message was the same: "Things sure aren't like they used to be," he would write. And then, after 25 years, when the annual greeting came, the handwriting on the envelope was different, as was the message. Myron had died.

Illness and death were part of my daily life during January, February, and March 1945. Mile after mile we continued an eastward trek into Germany, passing through towns and villages whose names I never knew. Although the shoes we wore provided some protection against the cold, snow, and ice, exposure to cold and moisture took its toll and swelled my right foot beyond shoe size. Frostbite began to set in. As my foot swelled, it was being squeezed tighter and tighter and with every step the pain grew worse. There were moments when I wanted to scream, but didn't dare.

I had witnessed other men in our unit, incapacitated by weakness or illness, drop out of the marches. Some were left to die; others were shot. I didn't want to become another victim. My decision to remove the shoe and toss it over a nearby hedge was wrenching, but necessary. Leaving it at the scene would have drawn attention to me—the last thing I wanted. I wrapped my foot with the scarf I wore around my neck, the only winter garment I had left. It helped until it became saturated with melted snow that later froze.

Physical and emotional pain stalked me throughout my captivity. Hunger gnawed at my stomach and extended throughout my body. The bitter cold affected my feet, legs, hands, and arms. My joints ached when I tried to bend them. My fingertips and toes alternated between extreme pain and periods of numbness. Keeping them moving helped somewhat.

I've thought often about how I could lie night after night on snow and ice, absorb the mental torment and the rifle butts in my back, and yet survive. What made that possible?

I've wrestled with that and concluded it was probably a combination of youth, emotional strength, earlier physical conditioning, and a will to survive.

In addition to everything else, our captors' attitude toward us ranged from indifference to our plight to pleasure at our suffering. For some of them, we were the mice, they the cats, and our lives the trophy. To demonstrate their Nazi superiority, they paraded their American victims through the main streets in many towns. Surprisingly, I didn't find any great rejoicing by the residents of those towns who witnessed our misery. I saw no pride on their faces, heard no shouts of "Deutschland über alles!" Some, I suspect, were embarrassed; perhaps others felt guilt. Among the elderly in particular, I detected sorrow, and I saw an occasional tear.

Reprieve – Short-lived

AFTER WEEKS OF the walking and working routine, I arrived at the only prisoner of war camp I would be "privileged" to enter during my stay in Germany. I regarded it as a privilege because it offered us at least shelter, some food, and companionship. We bunked with American prisoners. One, from Texas, strummed "The Yellow Rose of Texas" constantly on a guitar; it was entertaining, for a while. Prohibited from talking while on the road, we were eager for conversation—but didn't have much of a chance; Stammlager XIIA in Limburg, Germany, was a haven that lasted only two days.

The bunks for prisoners were similar to those I saw later in pictures of concentration camps, crammed with the emaciated bodies of inmates. At the POW camp, the bunks were not particularly comfortable. Nevertheless, they provided a reprieve from the cold earth I had become accustomed to sleeping on. How different captivity might have been for me if I had been a registered POW rather than a slave laborer. Instead of starvation rations and constant exposure to the frigid temperatures, I would have had at least minimal shelter, heat, a bed, food, and conversation, the opportunity to talk to fellow prisoners without the constant fear of a rifle barrel striking my back.

For months, I had not seen my reflection in a mirror or even a piece of shiny metal, and when I finally saw myself, I was stunned. My cheeks, once full, were sunken. The skin on my face had turned orange. It was frightening. I knew nothing about jaundice or hepatitis and could only imagine the worst: that I had contracted a fatal disease.

The hair I had once worn in a wavy pompadour was gone, leaving barely a stubble, the result of the only "medical" treatment I had received during the months of captivity: the removal of my lice-infested hair. The lice—another enemy we had to deal with, less obvious but capable of driving us out of our minds—had left mementos, however: scars and pockmarks that dotted my body and have remained for years.

War in Europe Rages On; A New Threat to Survival

THE ALLIED INVASION that had begun on June 6, 1944, on the beaches of Normandy seemed destined to bring victory soon, an expectation shared by most everyone in the world. Even in my pocket of isolation, I could surmise from the frenzy among the German troops that things were not going well for them and that perhaps they probably knew that, too.

Because the Germans were now in retreat and had to move more rapidly, they herded us into railroad boxcars, popularly known as "forty and eights" — large enough for forty humans or eight horses. Each car had one sliding door, no windows, no vents, no light.

How many more than forty we were, I don't know, but I estimated that we were between seventy and eighty. We were stacked, body lodged against body like sardines in a can, leaning but unable to find sitting space to spread out. Those able to squeeze to a sitting position were buried under falling bodies surrounding them.

Once a day the door slid open, and guards tossed pieces of bread into the "den." We clamored, clawed, and pushed our way to each fragment. We didn't take the time to savor our "quarry," devouring it as quickly as we snared it.

Adding to the intolerable conditions, our captors provided us with no sanitary facilities. We used what helmets we could find for body excretions, with no way to dispose of the contents. It was cold and damp inside the boxcar, the air putrid, my body stiff and uncomfortable. These conditions persisted for six days and nights. How much longer could I endure?

Fights were common. Each man existed for himself. Physical strength in each of us had waned, which probably kept more of us from being killed by our own hands, but some died. Some lost their minds. We went through a mental transformation. We had become a pack of animals. Only the fittest survived.

While imprisoned in the boxcar, I remember peering through a knothole or crack and seeing a US B-17 bomber was blown out of the sky. There was a puff of smoke, flames, and in seconds it was gone. With that image came a sickening feeling of defeat. In afterthought, I reflected on the lost lives of the airmen, the families they left, and the way the news would be delivered to their loved ones. I felt depressed, desperate, and helpless.

Finally, on the sixth day, the massive door slid back, revealing daylight and fresh air. It took a while to adjust. Herded like cattle, we were massed into marching units, guards posted to the right and to the left. With my right foot exposed, sore and frozen, and prodded by the guards, I set off with the others. The weather was bitter and I had only enough clothing left to cover my body. My thin jacket and trousers—the same Army clothes in which I had entered combat—were torn and filthy. I had been shorn of winter outer garments months earlier.

A Desperate Plan for Escape

I HAD OFTEN thought that escape would be the only way to survive, and if there were ever a time to do so, it was then, during this march. I don't recall anything heroic about it, simply a move made in desperation. I saw the opportunity and decided to take a chance.

With two others marching nearby, I devised a simple plan. The guards were spaced sufficiently far apart to allow for blind spots. If we could be beyond their sight for at least five seconds, we could make a break. As we rounded a curve in the road, opportunity struck. With a nod of the head and a motion of the hand to the left, I signaled the other two to throw themselves over a hedgerow. They did, and we were out of sight of the guards' watchful eyes for the first time in three months. Had we been spotted making our break, we would have been shot. And had the guards noticed three open spots in the ranks, some would have returned to search for the missing prisoners. That they didn't suggested to us that the others closed ranks, shielding our escape.

Because I had difficulty walking, I began to alternate between stumbling on two legs and crawling on hands and knees. We were heading toward a town we had passed through earlier; I learned later that it was Reichenbach, some 270 miles from Marvie, Belgium, where I had been captured.

As we approached the town, the sounds of activity became louder. The section we entered was residential, with small, neat homes; the land beyond, rural and peaceful. The rumble of engines and the clatter of heavy mobile equipment filled the air. Such sounds conflicted with this pastoral setting; they were the sounds of the battlefield. We had in fact entered a staging area for Nazi troops. Military vehicles and personnel filled the streets. We slunk through back alleys, careful to avoid the attention of soldiers who seemed to be everywhere. If we had been sighted, we'd have been shot.

We found ourselves in a secluded area, and stared at a house before us. Guided by instinct, I told the others I felt it was a "safe house." They didn't know whether to trust my instincts, but went along with the plan. We approached the entrance, I knocked cautiously, and a young man came to the door. We could see that his first instinct was to slam the door, but he hesitated as I tried to explain who we were—which was probably obvious to him and risky for us.

Our appearance must have shocked him. We were in terrible physical condition and the few articles of clothing we wore were filthy and in tatters. He summoned an older man and woman from inside, and fortune took over. Years earlier, the older couple had spent some time in Pittsburgh, and retained good memories of America and Americans. They recognized the US emblem on my jacket. Miraculously, we had come to a house of compassionate Germans!

"Why'd you pick that house?" one of the men asked later. I can't explain if it was instinct, logic, or just plain luck. In all likelihood, had I chosen another house, we would have been exposed to nearby German soldiers and shot. They were no longer taking prisoners.

With obvious trepidation and risking their own lives as they took action that would have branded them as traitors, the family drew us inside. We stared. It was the first time in many months that we had been in someone's home. Stuffed chairs, tables, wall hangings, and curtains were strange, comforting sights. Foremost in our thoughts, however, was food. We hadn't eaten in days. Sensitive to the obvious, they offered us some hot soup with a small piece of meat in it. I devoured it in seconds, and the sensation that followed was a quiet, subdued ecstasy. The memory of that soup would have to last another several days.

Our conversation, in English, was cordial yet cautious. They explained that with a German command post nearby, they couldn't risk sheltering us. Instead, the elderly couple drew us a map directing us through some back alleys leading to what they thought was an abandoned barn. The sounds of shellfire were near enough for us to realize we were not far from Allied lines, and we would be content to hole up in the barn. With what little strength remained in our bodies, we left the house, crawling through the alleys and narrowly avoiding the German soldiers who seemed to appear at every turn.

We followed the map and reached the barn; pulling ourselves up some steps, we landed in the hayloft.

The next morning, we heard something stir below and realized the building was not deserted. Pushing aside the hay, I peered through a crack in the floor. There, directly below, was a German soldier squatting on a stool, milking a cow. The vision of the top of his body, clad in long, white, heavy underwear, and black boots and suspenders is still clear in my memory.

As I tried to get a clearer view, some pieces of hay slipped through the opening and fell toward the soldier. My breathing suspended, I watched intently to see where the hay would land—if it fell in front of him, he would realize someone was up in the loft. That almost certainly would have led to our being discovered and killed. It fell behind him! The milking complete, he left the barn.

We lingered in the barn for two more days. During what must have been the second night, we heard the sounds of moving vehicles mingling with voices. By morning, a bewildering quiet had settled over the town. The Germans had pulled out.

From my position in the hayloft, I had a partial view of a narrow alley leading to the street. At one point, I thought I saw a few GI helmets darting past. I thought it might be a delusion—until I saw a jeep with a familiar white star on its hood. Skeptical of my report, my companions nevertheless agreed to descend from the hayloft, and the three of us literally crawled and rolled down the narrow alley. We at last came into the view of astonished but welcoming members of the American Third Armored Division.

The months of starvation, beatings, and exposure were over. Relief surged over me, but I was too weak to convey my feelings to my fellow soldiers. I lay there motionless for what must have been several minutes, not knowing how to react.

We were the first Americans the Third Armored Infantry had come across as they battled eastward across Germany. Obviously emaciated and ill, we became beneficiaries of their largesse. Of all that they fed us, I remember most the delectable, rich chocolate. That was probably the worst thing they could have given us. The sweetness made me sick! They tried to cram whatever they could get into me. I gagged, rejecting the foods my emotions clamored for.

CHAPTER 4:
LIFE RESTORED

Dark Memories Emerge

IT WAS ONLY as our liberators rushed me to an American field hospital to receive my first medical attention since falling into enemy hands, that I could begin to focus on the condition I was in. I had not realized how badly deteriorated and infected my body had become during the torturous months in captivity. (Years later, I recognized the similarities of that mobile emergency field hospital to the one portrayed during the Korean conflict on the TV program *M*A*S*H*.*)

The doctors worked diligently under difficult conditions, but because of the many illnesses and diseases I had contracted, I needed more intensive care. I was emotionally and intellectually weakened after months of deprivation, so my memories of being transferred to the First General Hospital in Liege, Belgium, and later to the First General Hospital in Paris are vague. I know I was given sulfa drugs and later had surgery to remove the infected bottoms of my feet. In the second week of April 1945, my departure for the United States was delayed because of an uncontrollable high fever.

Months later, in post-war civilian life, in an isolation unit of a hospital in Belleville, New Jersey, I learned that the fever I had contracted was undulant fever. A wise doctor, attempting to identify the disease, asked me many

questions about my service overseas and my experiences
as a prisoner. He zeroed in on the incident where we had
been locked in the barn for the night and where fellow
soldier Myron Barringer had squirted milk directly into
my mouth from the cow's udder. Bingo! The infection, a
disease with origins in the Mediterranean region, can be
contracted from unpasteurized cow's milk.

April 1945: Hospitalized in Paris, I seized my first opportunity to
write to Mom and Dad—light on details, heavy on emotion.

Had that discovery been made while I had been
hospitalized in Paris, I might have reached American
shores earlier. The raging fevers, aching joints, and
general debilitation caused by the undulant fever
delayed my return to the United States. During
captivity, I had been too busy fighting to stay alive to
dwell on the symptoms, but for years to come the disease
would take its toll on my body.

In the hospital in Paris, we received the shocking news that President Franklin D. Roosevelt had died. For some there was profound sadness, the recognition of the loss of a great leader, the visionary who had rallied the Americans at home and the troops abroad to fight and destroy the Nazi scourge. Heads hung low in the hospital ward.

After a month of treatment in European hospitals, the doctors finally got my fever down so that I could be moved; and I was strapped in a hospital bed aboard a US military aircraft. Once in the air, I could see little but blue sky speckled with small white clouds. As the plane landed, I felt suspense and then a surge of relief. We were in America, at a small airfield in New York state. Months earlier I could not have envisioned what it would feel like to finally reach home. I closed my eyes momentarily in prayer, and then, eager to see and confirm that I was indeed in America, stared at the countryside and the airport personnel on the ground. I whispered to myself, "Yeah, this is America."

> *Those little white clouds I saw through the airplane*
> *window hang vividly in my memory. They symbolized a*
> *reawakening. It was as though I had crossed a dateline.*
> *In the past, the war became history; ahead, the future*
> *loomed before me.*

Transported by ambulance to the military's Halloran General Hospital in Staten Island, New York, I tried to think of what might lie ahead. There were no clues. I was entering a new world and I would spend the next nine months—more than half of it bedridden—thinking, and not able to erase the memories of incidents that occurred and people I encountered during combat and captivity.

I was isolated upon arrival because of the possibility of contagious disease and the need for intensive care. A stream of doctors, nurses, and attendants paraded through my room, taking blood, infusing blood and other fluids, and giving me what must have been at least a dozen pills a day.

It wasn't surprising that as the doctors examined me, I heard again and again the words "anemic," "malnutrition," "no appetite," and "must gain weight." I had weighed in at just 89 pounds, down from 155, and had contracted more than 20 diseases, infections, and other disabilities. But with all the fluids and pills I ingested, little room was left for food.

When I was finally well enough to see family and friends, my parents were first. They had lived for three months in anguish and fear after receiving the first telegram from the War Department that reported me missing in action and the events leading up to my capture. My mother had suffered a nervous breakdown, endured the months of uncertainty, and, as she told me during that first hospital visit, had turned to God for support. She also described her mother's intuition when she "recognized" the ring on the telephone announcing my return to the States. She knew before reaching for the phone that it was from me.

When they arrived on their first visit to Halloran, my parents were shocked at my appearance and unable to recognize me at first. I was overjoyed to see Momma and Poppa, but the effects of medication prevented me from responding as my emotions urged. I was placid and able to offer little more than a weak smile. Other visiting relatives and friends walked by the room; my altered physical appearance also made it impossible for them to recognize me. My facial characteristics had changed. My once-full head of hair had diminished to a light fuzz; my cheeks were sunken; my face was pallid and wan; and I was incapable of forming a genuine smile. When my hair later started to grow in, the color changed periodically, possibly because of the tremendous amounts of medication I was receiving. At one stage, my hair was a brilliant purple (a hue uncommon until introduced in the '90s by Chicago Bulls basketball star Dennis Rodman).

The illnesses and ailments I sustained during my months as a prisoner were numerous. As the months of hospitalization rolled on, I recorded each medical condition as one might chart new adventures. The list, sufficient to titillate a first-year medical student, included severe malnutrition (which itself had made a welcoming environment for other illnesses), beriberi, typhoid fever, undulant fever, trench or relapsing fever, hepatitis, frozen feet and hands, trench foot, bronchitis, gastroenteritis, enterocolitis, duodenitis, anemia, arthritis, back injury, acute pyoderma on my hands and legs, acute sinusitis, and possibly a few others.

At night, I was lonely in my hospital room. During the day, I saw only doctors (many of them), nurses, and family members; and pills, pills and more pills. Nurses frequently arrived to draw my blood for analysis and later infuse blood to restore the loss. That would change when I became well enough to join others in the hospital's ward.

Skilled medical care and rest began to reverse the extreme bodily deterioration I had suffered, and after a couple of months I was ready to join the society of sick and wounded.

Of course, emotional scars—the memories of torment and isolation—remained. My move from isolation to a ward was a major step forward in the healing process. I had long since given up the ideals of privacy, and sought a reconnection with humanity.

Ten months of hospitalization; illnesses, fevers,
injuries, and an emaciated body take time to heal.
This partial list of the twenty-six illnesses I contracted
during the war was recorded in my little brown book.

It took me a while to adjust to being in the ward. Quiet and subdued, I didn't connect with the other patients during the first couple of days, but then that started to change. We started to exchange information, asking one another which units we had served in and what experiences we had gone through. The camaraderie I felt with the others in the ward, as strange as it may seem, was greater than what I had felt in combat or captivity.

When I arrived on the ward and the others learned I had been a slave laborer—an experience different from their own—they asked a lot of questions about what I had endured and how I had escaped.

I also learned what some of my fellow patients had gone through, how they were wounded, their views on the enemy and the war, and about the Germans they had encountered.

Our conversation often turned to the lives that lay ahead. What were we going to do after our discharge from the Army? I heard lots of big ideas and ambitious plans, but also just the anticipated joy of being reunited with family and friends.

Often, the wife of a patient in a nearby bed would come over to talk to me. Her husband, Harry, had leukemia—an incurable disease—and I believe our conversations offered her some relief from the emotional pain she was suffering. Believing that a cure was imminent, she held out hope. That cure or treatment did not happen soon enough, and Harry passed away. He was a fine man, and I missed him.

Sleepless Nights, Haunting Visions

WHILE I HAD endured the darkness of night during my captivity, I remember the pain, both physical and mental, that it induced. "Bunking down" variably on hard cold ground, or ice or snow, I had rarely been able to sleep. Pain raged throughout my body, from head to foot. My emotions were torn by the realization that I could do nothing to relieve the pain. Nor could I envision an end to this kind of torment, and I thought about death. How long before the starvation and exposure would take my life?

Many of these episodes of anxiety, visions from the battle zone and captivity, haunted me at night in the hospital. Though I was now in a safe environment, many nights it was impossible for me to simply doze off. When I did sleep, I would often dream I was back on a barren field, lying on the hard, frozen earth.

Crowding my mind were images. I saw the German tank-like vehicles we encountered while searching for the American battle lines; in my imagination, it was a monster waiting to devour me. I saw that American plane blown out of the sky and felt the sorrow that had consumed me at the sight. I relived the squalor of my confinement for six days and nights in the German railroad cattle car, starved, cold, and crushed by other captives. These returning visions often made me curl up in bed, desiring security.

So many events clustered and darted around in my mind during those mostly sleepless nights. Transferring from my private room to the ward didn't help much. The visions continued to reappear, but some of them were pleasant. Many of my nighttime memories, occurring time and again, centered around two encounters with Germans who were not typical Nazi supporters.

I couldn't forget the elderly couple in the house in Reichenbach where my instinct had told me that I and my fellow escapees would find refuge. I remembered the sympathetic expressions on their faces when they recognized the US medallion on my jacket and how they took us in, fed us, and helped guide us to safety. It was a vision, hazy at times, that would emerge frequently as I attempted to sleep. Why I trusted my instinct, I'll never know. Had that couple not visited Pittsburgh and liked Americans, they more than likely would have led the German soldiers to discover us, resulting in our deaths.

The German sergeant was an ill-defined image that occasionally I thought of while lying awake. I don't remember his face, only that I stood there peering down into a foxhole, staring at a German helmet as the shrapnel from American artillery landed around me.

I revisited the scene frequently. My memory of it was clear: the burning tank, the long row of machine gun-equipped bunkers preventing an escape. I wrestled with the question of what must have been going through this German sergeant's mind as our conversation shifted. It became difficult for me to think we were enemies and that our assignments were to kill one another.

"It's not PROPAGANDA"

Patient Relates Experiences Inside German Labor Camps

By Pfc. Harry Schwartz

Look at the tired, half-starved face of Pfc Robert Max, and you'll see why the European war may be over but the Nazis will never be forgotten - or forgiven. I don't mean the photo accompanying this article. That shows a Pfc Max after two months of treatment at American hospitals abroad and one week at Halloran. For how he looked after losing 45 pounds in 90 days of German prison camps, consult any of the atrocity photographs recently released by the Army. The Nazi starvation method achieves the same pictorial effects on all of its victims - including those who manage to survive.

Max and six other Americans were taken prisoner by 100 Germans after a pitched battle in Belgium.

"We thought we were dead ducks," Robert said, "but they weren't letting us off that easy. First they stripped our winter clothing off us, leaving only flimsy garments. The weather was freezing. Then they marched us across Belgium and Luxemburgh - about a quarter of the way into Germany. We made stops, of course, but not because the Germans thought we might be tired. It was to put us to work at labor camps where the normal working day was a 10-hour stretch - although we often had to work all through the night."

Robert and the others had to lift and carry heavy tracks and lumber as far as 4 or 5 miles. A weakened physical condition was no excuse from hard labor. So the labor casualties began to pile up. "We spent many evenings burying our dead," Max said. "Malnutrition, lack of medical care and beatings took a terrible toll. God! I'll never forget the time one of my buddies, weakened by long undernourishment, collapsed under a load

he was carrying.

"A few of us ran to his aid, but the guards jabbed us in the ribs with their guns. We were too weak and helpless to challenge them. While we stood by, the swine rolled our buddy over on his face, kicked him a few times until he lay still. They left him there, dying in the snow."

Robert and his fellow-prisoners moved on from camp to camp through bitter Winter weather. He contracted frozen feet and hands which became progressively worse; but he received no medical attention. Although he had never had any illusions about the Nazis, he was startled at the depths of treachery and inhuman brutality to which they could go. "Don't think they didn't paint large red crosses on their munitions and supply trucks," he said. "I saw them, myself."

Each labor camp had their own special feature in diet and refined methods of torture. "At Prum Labor Camp, we were fed 6 whole crackers, 1 inch in diameter, and a piece of cheese. That was our meal for a full day. At Gerolstine, we got a little variety - a canteen cup of flour and water and 1/6 of a loaf of brown bread per day, by itself here we got a taste of Hell, itself. There were numerous beatings, and men died daily from sickness and disease. I don't know how I lived through it all, but the desire to return home some day gave me the will to hang on."

Then came the news that the Americans were closing in. Our captors went into action. They packed us into boxcars that normally held 35 people. 70 or 80 of us were jammed into each car and we were boxed in that way for 6 days and nights. There were no latrines, so our helmets had to serve.

Finally, Robert and his buddies

were taken from the train, formed into columns, and driven further into the heart of Germany. "We learned that the Americans were not far away. Two of my buddies and I decided to make a break for it. We knew that capture meant death but we were desperate.

"It was late in the afternoon. We had already arranged a signal for our escape. The guard was marching up ahead. We waited until we heard 'Column right march!' That was the signal. As the guards swung to the right, we made a dash for it, to the left. We hopped over the fence in a nearby field and dropped flat behind it. The column marched on as though we were still part of it."

Robert and his companions lay in the grass behind the fence until nightfall. Then they prowled through the streets of the nearby town, looking for food. One German family, in a small house, gave them food. "We didn't know whether it was pity for us or fear of approaching American troops that made them feed us. But there was no time to wonder, so we ate hurriedly and hid in a barn up the road for three days and nights.

"On March 29, four days after our break, I awoke and dragged myself to a peephole in the barn. I saw GI helmets and for a moment, I thought my empty belly was making me see things. But as they came closer, the three of us stumbled into the sunlight, into the arms of American troops. We laughed, and then we cried with joy."

The men were taken by ambulance to a hospital where Robert's frozen feet were treated for the first time. "They were in bad shape. Dead flesh had to be cut away and sulfa applied before the healing process began.

Robert spent five weeks in European hospitals and now he is at Halloran where he enjoys the finest medical care - medical care that was denied him by the Germans, as they have done to so many others.

HALLORAN

This article, which ran in Halloran General Hospital's newspaper after I underwent three initial months of treatment in European hospitals, was the first I spoke about Nazi atrocities involving American soldiers.

Our missions, our ideologies had been totally different; and yet, I had felt a bonding with this soldier. He was unique, unlike the others who inflicted on us the pain, suffering, and starvation that accompanied slave labor. I considered it a miracle that I had encountered a German soldier who spoke English and possessed humanitarian instincts.

Other images haunted me: an abundance of dead bodies; the armed, white-clad German soldiers poised over us as we ascended from our hideout in the shack; the photo of the German sergeant's family, evidence of his conviction that they would all be in New York City "next year." These were mostly darting images, reminding me again and again how close I had come to death.

I've often been asked if I ever gave up hope. My answer, hesitant at times, is no. "I always had three options," I've said. "One, the war would end and I'd be free; two, I might find an opportunity to escape; and three, my spirits were boosted at night as I thought about, tasted and smelled the foods — 84 in all — that I would again enjoy in post-war America."

Flashbacks while lying awake were also common for me. Some of these dated to my pre-war years — years when, methodically, I "took inventory" of each day's activity before dozing off at night. How did I do at school today? What about athletics? Music? Social life? These thoughts about my pre-war years became interwoven with my wartime memories.

While hospitalized in Belgium and France, I speculated on what life would be like and what I would do in the post-war world. I wanted to resume my education, but for some reason at Cornell University, not Ohio University, where I had planned to enter my junior year. But, a mysterious, compelling voice emerged from the clouds (the clouds that I gazed at from the plane window as we crossed the Atlantic Ocean), and urged me to return to Ohio University. Following that emotional impulse altered the rest of my life.

As one of very few American soldiers who had been captured in the Battle of the Bulge, subjected to atrocities, and survived and escaped Nazi captivity, I was interviewed on network radio by Stan Lomax, a popular newscaster in the 1930s and '40s. A group of students from the Hillel Foundation (a national Jewish student organization) happened to tune in to the broadcast and began to listen more intently when they heard me say, "I'm going to return to Ohio University."

When I did return, word spread through the membership that the soldier they had heard on the radio was indeed on campus. Hillel was about to hold its election of officers, someone nominated me, and sight unseen, I became president of the organization. As a neophyte, I asked Shirley Biller — the Hillel member who would have become president had I not returned — if she would work with me during my tenure in office. Her favorable nod became a partnership — and later a marriage lasting nearly 68 years, until her death in July 2015.

My return to Ohio University also saw the beginnings of my career, including business initiatives that derived from an urge to serve in some productive way and to aid others, many facing hardship. I fulfilled this

urge through existing social service organizations
as well as those I created. I viewed my drive as a
subconscious response to having survived against almost
insurmountable odds in warfare. In Hebrew, this is
expressed as "gemilut chasadim," or "bestowing acts of
loving kindness." For me it became a way of life, and for
Shirley and me, it was the most important work we did
for the next 68 years.

Welcome Back to the World

ATHLETICS AND MUSIC had been central to my life before the war, and both had an effect on my military career.

Music of the 1930s and '40s — particularly big band swing and orchestras that sometimes included up to 18 skilled musicians playing a host of instruments — was a major part of the world I lived in, both a fan and as a musician playing alto saxophone and clarinet.

When I was just starting out, at age 16, I led a small group. We rehearsed one tune, Glenn Miller's "In the Mood," for many months in preparation for a show to be produced by our athletic club to raise money to buy uniforms. We had problems, though. The Glenn Miller Orchestra had 16 musicians; we had only five, and I had just started taking lessons. For those many months, we practiced the same melody in my family's living room every Saturday. It drove my mother frantic. The sounds were dreadful. Fortunately, though, the show never came off, and we found other ways of raising money for uniforms.

But that was not the end of my music career. I continued taking saxophone and clarinet lessons, and influenced by the many professional musicians whose careers I followed, I started to play with local bands in New Jersey, and later in Ohio during my time at college.

In the hospital, pleasant memories of those days came flooding back, mixing together with my recent painful war experiences.

I recalled our band's performance at a party, when a dancing couple brushed past me and blew the sheet music off my music stand. On my hands and knees, I chased the pages across the floor, crawling through the dancers' feet, tripping them as I sought my target. The other band members broke out in laughter, and the dancers applauded as I made my way back to the bandstand—the loudest and longest applause of the night.

My career blossomed when I landed the first time at Ohio University. Musicians in Athens were the next best thing to the top professionals. Dressed in tuxedoes, as were most musicians in America's leading bands, we were a striking group. I was earning $50 a week, which helped with some of my incidental college expenses. When I joined the union, local 179 in Marietta, Ohio, I became a card-carrying professional musician.

It was that experience that somehow became part of my record when I enlisted, and it was responsible for my being inducted into the military swing band at Fort Dix in New Jersey. How different Army life would have been had I remained with the band at Fort Dix and not ventured off to basic training to become an Army rifleman.

I could have stayed; it had been arranged. It was one of the many choices I made, the kind we all make in life—choices that often determine who and what we become.

That was a pivotal moment in my life. Now, as I approach my 94th birthday, I realize that the choice I made then shaped the next 70 years. The stored memories of combat and captivity, the deprivation of life's offerings, and my near-death encounters greatly influenced my urge to devote my post-war years to meeting human needs through personal service. Had I chosen music over combat, my life would probably have taken a whole different trajectory.

During some of those sleepless hours at Halloran General Hospital, I remembered the emphasis I placed on bodily strength and stamina, and how they contributed to my survival. Smaller than most, I worked harder, and set the record for push-ups in my Army unit.

In my teens, I hung out with a group of athletes and played organized baseball, basketball, and football. Undersized—I stood 5 feet, 4 inches tall and weighed 135 pounds—I had always been sensitive to how I looked and felt. To bulk up, I took the Charles Atlas Dynamic Tension Bodybuilding course. It worked, and while I was still on the small side, I became stronger, faster, more agile, and more secure, bowling over the opposition on the football field with "chop blocks" (throwing one's body at the runner's legs—allowed then, but later prohibited) and cutting down big guys who outweighed me by 50 to 60 pounds.

In my final football season before heading for college, we played the Boonton Panthers in their home stadium. The four smallest players on our Vailsburg Braves team, including me, were the first on the field for the pre-game warmup. The stadium erupted in laughter and opposing fans yelled chiding remarks, calling us "Singer Midgets" (a reference to a traveling troupe of entertainers). Their attitude changed as the game got under way!

I quarterbacked that day. We received, took the kickoff, and threw a pass to a fleet receiver who raced to the end zone. Though it's not done today, the pass on kickoff was allowed. We scored the extra point and led 7 to 0, which turned out to be the final score. Outweighed but not out-fought, we managed to hold them scoreless.

The result stunned the crowd and both teams. It was the first and last time I ever heard applause from players and patrons alike. After the game, a hat was passed around the stadium to pay the players. I never played again.

When I was admitted to Halloran General Hospital, I weighed just 89 pounds, a full 40 pounds below my pre-Charles Atlas weight as a teenager, and 65 pounds less than when I had been inducted into the Army. Bedridden, I thought a lot about my previous athletic pursuits and remembered how important athletics and physical conditioning had been during my developing years.

Baseball was my favorite sport, and as a kid I dreamed of someday playing for the New York Yankees. On my third birthday, my 11-year-old brother bought me a Yankees uniform and a bat, baseballs, and a glove.

Our backyard had a fence, perhaps 50 feet from "home plate." I don't remember how many home runs I scored, but I hit a lot of balls over that fence. My brother was a good pitcher. Playing with him in the yard was good conditioning for my teenage years with our local team, the Vailsburg Braves. As a swift and agile left and center fielder, I ran down many balls. My reputation, though, was "good field, no hit."

It was not surprising that I reacted positively to the Army's physical training. I know with certainty that my early years of playing sports, combined with the physical training I received in the military, were key to my having survived an ordeal that took the lives of thousands. As I lay in bed month after month, remembrances of my youth also led me to believe that perhaps I had escaped death to serve others in useful ways.

A Grateful Nation Cheers Its Returning Veterans

REBUILDING MY BODY required nourishment, and it wasn't coming fast enough in the hospital. Something more was needed, and that something turned out to be Grossinger's, the fabled Catskill Mountains resort in upper New York state. Owner Jennie Grossinger, her family, and the hotel staff provided selfless support for returning American servicemen. They regularly opened their doors and their hearts to veterans, offering the full range of facilities and the fabulous food for which they were famous. When the Grossinger family again offered to host a soldier in need of rest and relaxation (and in my case, weight gain), my name was at the top of the list.

After the chaplain at Halloran made the arrangements, I was off for a week of rehabilitation with my own hospital "press agent," Harry Schwartz. Anyone who ever vacationed in the "Borscht Belt"—so-called because of its popularity among Jews—knows it was home to many vacation establishments noted for sumptuous meals in spectacular dining halls and was the training ground for many of America's leading comedians.

At Grossinger's, the fare was lavish, luscious, and certain to add pounds to any frame. That was the idea behind the prescription, and it worked. Hostess Karla Grossinger treated me like a visiting dignitary, and I was asked to write an article in the resort newsletter, *The Tattler.*

Summer 1945: Three months along on the road to recovery at Halloran General Hospital on Staten Island, New York, my experience as a slave laborer in Nazi Germany was revealed for the first time. With my hair grown back and a smile on my face, happier days lay ahead.

As I was the only American soldier visiting Grossinger's at the time, I drew a lot of attention, particularly from mothers looking for a "nice Jewish boy" to marry their daughters. But I wasn't ready for marriage yet.

At the hospital after a week of ceaseless gorging, I found I had put on an astounding amount of weight—enough for the staff and chaplain to prescribe another week, and Grossinger's extended its hospitable arms to me a second time. I put on more pounds and progressed on the road to renewed health.

With Japan's official surrender on September 2, 1945, World War II came to an end. It was a great time to be alive and in America. The nation treated its returning warriors as heroes. In New York City, veterans had access to radio broadcasts, Broadway shows, and sporting events at Madison Square Garden. I even was given my own weekly box seats at Carnegie Hall—home of the New York Philharmonic Orchestra— donated by a generous family who gave up their tickets in order to provide returning servicemen with quality musical events. I especially enjoyed those concerts, which I attended with others from the hospital ward. Before each event, in our bright maroon bathrobes, we were recognized as heroes by the announcers and cheered enthusiastically by audiences. On network radio, broadcaster Stan Lomax interviewed me as a survivor of German slave labor (the interview that led to my becoming president of the Hillel Foundation at Ohio University, and ultimately to my meeting Shirley, who would become my wife). Earlier, I had appeared as a game show contestant along with my brother Lester, an Army sergeant on his way to the war that was then still being fought in the Pacific. I correctly identified jazz singer Mildred Bailey as the vocalist in a mystery entertainer contest and won a bunch of silver dollars.

A One-Man Search and an Improbable Ending

POST-COMBAT LIFE for me had taken a dramatic turn, each day filled with adventure. How different from my months of captivity, when time had lost relevance. Then there had been just daylight and darkness, fading into one another, indistinct. Family and civilian life were absent during this time as my sole focus narrowed to just surviving one more day. It was difficult to reconcile the past with the present.

Though they have slipped below my everyday attention and moved to the recesses of my mind, and are only occasionally rekindled at night, my memories of the war linger to this day and I will never forget them.

Once I reached the United States and my health improved slightly, I learned what my family had experienced while I was a prisoner of war.

After I was reported missing in action in the Battle of the Bulge, I had become the object of a dedicated one-man search. Earlier my parents had received the following Western Union telegram from the Adjutant General in Washington, DC:

The secretary of war desires me to express his deep regret that your son Private First Class Robert R. Max has been reported missing in action since four January in Belgium. If further details or other information are received, you will be promptly notified.

Well, further details were not available. One month and then a second went by and still no new information. After my return to America, I learned, that my family's assumption at that time was that I must have been killed. Families with members in combat dreaded the ring of the doorbell and the delivery of a Western Union telegram. It invariably meant devastating news. Hands trembled as the envelope was opened. I can only imagine how my folks must have felt as they read the initial telegram.

Meanwhile, a company clerk in an administrative unit who saw my name on a "missing-in-action report" issued a request to other communications specialists in the area to alert him if my name appeared on any further lists. This communications officer, through the area's radio network, ultimately received the startling news that I was alive and hospitalized.

The communications officer who sought my status was my brother Lester—one of many thousands of American soldiers in the area. What were the odds of my own brother being the one to discover I was alive?

While I had no idea that Lester was even stationed in the European theater of operations, I later discovered that it was he who engineered the one-man search for his younger brother, resulting in the unimaginable coincidence that alerted him to my survival.

With eight years separating us, my brother treated me almost as a father would treat a son. His investigation, his probing, and eventually his discovery that I had returned to Allied hands was typical of our relationship. It was the same feeling that prompted his purchasing monthly US war savings bonds for me during our service in the Army.

On April 26, 1945, following months of determined effort to learn where I was, he wrote:

> *Dear Mom and Pop,*
>
> *I'm so happy I could cry. Just a few hours ago, I received a letter from European Theater of Operations Headquarters telling me that Bob was okay. Here is the first paragraph of that letter:*
>
> Dear Cpl. Max:
>
> I am very happy to report that your brother, Pfc. Robert R. Max, ASN 15311529, was liberated by advancing forces on 4 April 1945 after having been previously reported as missing in action on 4 January 1945…
>
> *(The original letter, dated from Germany, April 26, 1945, now discolored and tattered on the edges, was shown and read in July 2015 during a filming of my life story by the United States Holocaust Memorial Museum.)*

Germany...April 26, 1945

Dear Mom & Pop:

I'm so happy I could cry. Just a few hours ago I received a letter from European Theater of Operations Headquarters telling me that Bob was okay. Here is the first paragraph of the letter:

"Dear Cpl Max:

I am very happy to report that your brother, Pfc Robert R. Max, ASN 15511529, was liberated by our advancing forces from a German prisoner of war camp on 4 April 1945 after having been previously reported as missing in action on 4 January 1945."

I had previously written Bob's company clerk, and his answer was written before the report of Bob's liberation was received at 6th Armored Division headquarters. So, along with the letter from ETO headquarters, came a letter from 6th Armored, dated 8 days earlier, stating that there was no further news of Bob.

The letter read, in part, "Pfc Max was with his Company as they attacked enemy positions about 1½ miles Northeast of Marvie, Belgium, on 4 January 1945. An enormous amount of enemy artillery, mortar, and small arms fire was encountered, and squads and individuals became separated at times because of the necessity of seeking protection from this fire. After this engagement Pfc Max was not present. A search was made of the vicinity, but he could neither be found nor accounted for, and up to the present date there has been no further information on your brother."

Well, further information came today and I don't think I've ever received anything that made me happier. Captain Bodrogi informed me that all prisoners of war for more than 30 days are returned to the United States. If that is so, there is an excellent chance of your seeing him soon. I wish I could too.

If he is going to be reassigned, I'd like to get him into my outfit. Better still, I'd like to see him stay in the States. I intend asking Captain Bodrogi's advise tomorrow.

What can I add to a letter like this? I'm overjoyed and can't think of another thing right now. I know how happy you both must be and I know now that God must have heard your prayers. All I can say is that we have a lot to be thankful for.

Call Diane when you receive this letter. I'm too excited to write any more tonight. When I calm down, I'm going to write Bob at Central Postal Directory, APO 640, U.S. Army. And within a few days I'm going to send you the letters for safekeeping. Right now I want to enjoy them myself.

Write soon and God bless you. Love to Ruthie.

Lester

April 1945: The original letter from my brother Lester to my parents, bringing them the startling news that the son they had feared dead for over four months was in fact alive.

In a letter sent to Lester eight days earlier by my unit, the 6th Armored Division, the company clerk had written:

> *...Pfc. Max was with his Company as they attacked*
> *enemy positions about 1½ miles northeast of Marvie,*
> *Belgium. An enormous amount of enemy artillery,*
> *mortar, and small arms fire was encountered, and*
> *squads and individuals became separated...*

Lester went on to conclude his letter to our parents:

> *What can I add to a letter like this? I'm overjoyed and*
> *can't think of another thing right now. I know how*
> *happy you both must be, and I know now that God must*
> *have heard your prayers. All I can say is that we have a*
> *lot to be thankful for.*
>
> *I'm too excited to write any more tonight. When I*
> *calm down, I'm going to write Bob at Central Postal*
> *Directory, APO 640 US Army. And within a few days,*
> *I'm going to send you the letters for safekeeping. Right*
> *now, I want to enjoy them myself.*

On April 16, 1945, the official word to my parents had come from the Adjutant General in a telegram:

> *The Secretary of War desires me to inform you that*
> *your son, Pfc. Robert R. Max returned to military*
> *control 4 April 1945. Report further states however he is*
> *hospitalized in European area. New address and further*
> *information follow direct from hospital.*

There it was—official notification. The months of desperation and fear of the worst culminated in the relief and the joy that only a parent can feel; and, I might add, a brother whose concern matched that of my parents. I left military service on December 15, 1945.

Now I ask the question posed by so many who experienced the bitterness, fright, and frustration of war: Why was I spared when others perished?

The mysteries of birth, life and death, good fortune, and failure remain just that—not always answerable. There are events, though, that shape or redirect our lives.

The ribbon on the right has an Oak Leaf Cluster,
indicating a second issue of the Purple Heart award.

Just as life in America was permanently altered by World War II, so it was that my life, my outlook, and my fortunes would never be the same.

There are times when I cannot conceive that any of this happened:

I CANNOT CONCEIVE of lying night after night for three months, with no overcoat or gloves, on cold, hard ground—sometimes on snow or ice in sub-zero temperatures—always hungry, always thinking about food, and finding only brief moments of sleep.

I CANNOT CONCEIVE of standing above ground in the Ardennes Forest while my captors were protected in bunkers as American artillery shells exploded around us, sending a blizzard of shrapnel to the surrounding area.

I CANNOT CONCEIVE of my personal indifference to my surroundings—exposed to and surrounded by exploding artillery shells—as I talked and debated warfare with an English-speaking German sergeant.

I CANNOT CONCEIVE of the unlikely humanitarian behavior of this German soldier and his intentions (though later overturned) that I be sent to a POW camp and not be killed on the spot.

I CANNOT CONCEIVE of surviving six days of animalistic behavior, insanity, and death in a German railroad boxcar.

I CANNOT CONCEIVE that despite our escaping into a town that was a German military staging area (where recognition meant instant death), two comrades and I were not discovered.

I CANNOT CONCEIVE of my miraculous selection of a "safe house" for protection following escape; one occupied uniquely by an elderly couple who had visited America and admired Americans.

I CANNOT CONCEIVE that the first person to learn I was alive following my escape and rescue was my brother, a company clerk responsible for communications in another Army unit.

CHAPTER 5:
A NEW MISSION

A Civilian in a Strange New World

I WAS A CIVILIAN now in a strange new world. The people I knew, the clothes I wore, the food I ate, and the routines I followed were all different. My ten months of hospitalization had afforded me a lot of time to think, but the time alone with my thoughts had also generated uneasiness. A force I didn't understand seemed to be saying, "You were spared. Now do something about it." What the enemy had failed to achieve—my demise—became an impetus and challenge for me to make the rest of my life meaningful.

My transition from soldier to college, civilian, and married life provided countless opportunities for me to serve others; some by design, some by chance. Initially my efforts centered around the organized Jewish community; I became active in social service organizations, raised funds for charitable causes, and got involved in synagogue life. Later, my endeavors encompassed city, county, and state civic roles.

I also sought varied forms of expression, a natural result of being released from the constraints of military life. My search led to activities ranging from my designing and developing new products and businesses, to competing in (and winning!) the 50- and 100-meter dashes in a regional Senior Olympics contest, to writing music and lyrics for the album of the popular TV Western series *Bat Masterson*.

*On my wedding day, my brother Lester
(at right) wishes me a happy life.*

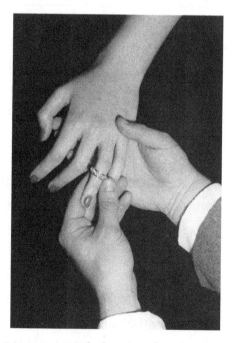

*May 9, 1948: The happiest day of my life,
as Shirley proffers her hand in marriage.*

For 53 years, the one activity I never engaged in was talking about my wartime experiences. I had locked them into the recesses of my mind and didn't think it mattered much to others. This all changed suddenly when my grandsons, then ages seven and nine, began to ask me difficult personal questions.

"Poppy, were you in the war?"

"What did you eat?"

"Where did you sleep?"

"Did you carry a gun?"

"Did you shoot anyone?"

"Did you kill anyone?"

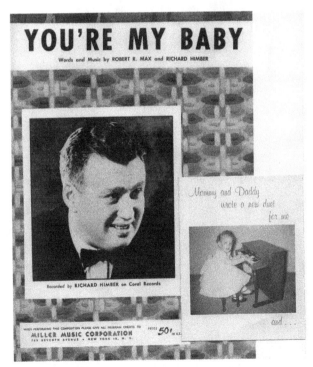

My daughter Wendy and her $45 piano inspired
me to write a popular song of the 1950s.

Spurred by my grandsons' curiosity, I realized it was time to release the stored memories. A weekend my wife and I spent with Holocaust survivor and Nobel laureate Elie Wiesel in 1988 gave me further incentive to speak out.

Grandson Xander at age seven, inspired by my story of combat and captivity, tries on "Poppy's" uniform.

Kofi Kwarteng, born and raised in Ghana and later an exchange student at Summit High School in New Jersey, became a member of our family. Here he is with his son, Maxime.

Every five years, Shirley and I took our family on vacation somewhere far away; this time to Canada. From left to right, our seven guys and a gal are grandson Zarek, son-in-law Bob Siegel, son Doug, daughter Wendy, and grandsons Tayson, Xander, Kyler, and Emerson.

The El-Hananys, an Israeli family we met and "adopted" during their time in America, have remained family for more than four decades.

On March 10, 1994, after unanimous support in the state legislature, New Jersey enacted a bill mandating that

Holocaust and genocide education be taught in the public schools.

When, as a survivor of Nazi atrocities, I was asked to share my war experiences with middle school and high school students, I felt I was finally ready to share my stories outside my own family.

When I spoke in classrooms, most of the students came well prepared; this was not storytelling time. Their questions revealed that the message had gotten through. They had an understanding of the horrors of war, and most importantly, of the dangers of ignoring the signs of an approaching genocide. They knew that six million Jews had been murdered during World War II and that the admonition to "never forget" was more than just a slogan. The purpose of my talks was to task them with the mission of serving as witnesses, to increase their awareness, and to urge them to speak out when they saw injustice or persecution. I believe that hearing the evidence from a survivor made them more committed to accepting the mission. Many wrote me letters afterward pledging to do so.

One high school student in particular stands out. He raised his hand, stood up, and asked, "Mr. Max, would you ever want to live through that experience again?"

It was a strange question. I had told them of the six days I was crammed with 70-80 other captives in a boxcar built to hold 40, with no place to sit or recline. I had described how we had become a pack of animals, scrambling and clawing for the few crusts of bread thrown into the car each morning. I told them that several of the men became mentally deranged and that some died.

I responded to the student, "Given a choice, I surely would not want to live through that again. But am I glad I had the experience and survived it? I'd say yes."

But why?

Perhaps it was because I learned a lot about human nature and my own will to survive. I had experienced first-hand how men could, under extreme conditions, change character and behavior.

Faith and Human Needs the Nazis Couldn't Shake

LIKE THOSE of many American Jews, my experiences during World War II would also forever change my identification with my faith. The Star of David and the mezuzah I defiantly wore around my neck next to my dog tags throughout the war became a talisman for me for the rest of my life, and a constant reminder of how precious my religious identity still is to me.

Shirley and I moved to Summit, New Jersey, in 1957. A short time later, Shirley established a section of National Council of Jewish Women, and I was invited to a meeting of the campaign cabinet of the local United Jewish Appeal. Within a year, I became chairman of this philanthropic organization, a role I held for 15 years, followed by another 47 years of raising funds for non-profit organizations that served public and human needs, including United Jewish Appeal, State of Israel Bonds, The United Way, and the The Jewish Historical Society of New Jersey.

In 1994, Shirley and I also led a group that established a Reconstructionist synagogue in Chatham, New Jersey. Inspired by the writings of Rabbi Mordecai Kaplan, founder of the Reconstructionist movement, we were particularly moved by his perspective on Judaism. He viewed it as "the evolving religious civilization of the Jewish people" and suggested that Judaism and its practices, while rooted in traditions, ought to reflect societal change. Jewish "civilization," in his view, was more than spirituality and religious practice; it encompassed language, music, the arts and drama, Israel, and customs of the times.

Shirley's cheerful look was like a beacon to me
for the sixty-seven years of our marriage.

Kaplan's ideas captured our minds, our imaginations, and our yearning for a religious experience more spiritually moving and in tune with the world we were living in.

As founding members of Congregation Beth Hatikvah, we were committed to providing a synagogue home for the practice of Reconstructionist Judaism. Our enthusiasm extended to our many guests, who came, explored, and were moved by what they saw and felt at the congregation's Shabbat evening services. Membership grew that first year.

In our second year, in recognition of Veterans Day, instead of a sermon during the Sabbath service, three members who were World War II veterans spoke to the congregation about their wartime experiences.

I wanted to sprint when the German sergeant said, "We have to kill you," but I had nowhere to run. Forty years later, at age sixty-four, I did—in a regional Senior Olympics staged by the JCC of Metrowest, New Jersey. I earned a gold medal in the 50-meter dash and a silver in the 100-meter dash.

I talked first, describing my combat, capture, and escape. Dr. Sidney Trubowitz was next. Sidney told of his experiences as assistant director of internal medicine at the US military's Halloran General Hospital, describing how each morning he had led a team of doctors and assistants on their rounds, visiting patients in each room.

Suddenly, Sidney paused. I rose from my seat, looked at him, and asked, "Sid, were you my doctor?" Later we compared the dates of his service and my hospitalization. They coincided. This coincidence was just one of many moments throughout my life that helped to convince me that the war had created a destiny, a path of service for me to follow. Although I had not been particularly observant before the war, service to the Jewish community and beyond became a major focus of my post-war life.

Two Bar Mitzvahs: A Second Chance for a Second Act

FOR JEWISH BOYS, preparing for their bar mitzvah is a milestone event. The ceremony at age 13 marks the transition from boy to man, when a youth becomes morally and ethically responsible for his decisions and actions. It is not an end of Jewish education, but the beginning of learning and participating in the Jewish community.

My own bar mitzvah at age 13 was memorable for a different reason. Our Reform synagogue did not follow the more traditional bar mitzvah practices common in Conservative and Orthodox congregations. As a bar mitzvah boy, I did not read from the Torah (the Old Testament) during the service; I only delivered the blessings before and after the reading of the Torah by the congregation's cantor. But a highlight of the service at Temple B'nai Jeshurun in Newark was the bar mitzvah boy's speech.

I anticipated this important occasion and wanted to share it with my non-Jewish friends. Growing up in the Vailsburg section of Newark, I did not experience the anti-Semitism that was prevalent in so many other neighborhoods at that time. Few of my closest friends were Jewish. It seemed appropriate to invite my buddies, and my parents agreed.

When the day of the ceremony finally arrived, I delivered my bar mitzvah speech in the traditional fashion. As soon as I finished, my friends jumped to their feet, whistled, and clapped! This was a shock to our congregation. Decorum and solemnity are an integral part of the Sabbath service, and I saw many adults look to the floor, shaking their heads in disapproval. I was embarrassed and my parents were upset, but it quickly blew over. After the service, I thanked each of my friends for coming. Months later, a friend invited me to attend Christmas Eve Midnight Mass at the Sacred Heart Church in Newark. My being Jewish never interfered with the respect and friendship my friends and I had for each other.

According to Psalms, during King David's time, the human lifespan stretched to the age of 70. Age 71 was considered to be the point of starting life over. A rationale developed using a simple mathematic equation: $70 + 13 = 83$, the age at which one is eligible for a second bar mitzvah.

Few Jewish men choose to go through the ceremony at that age. But imbued with the reality of my Jewish heritage, leadership of two Jewish congregations, the urging of my wife Shirley, and the support of our rabbi, Amy Small, I accepted the challenge to be a bar mitzvah "boy" a second time. It meant that I had to study and prepare to read Hebrew directly from the Torah—not an easy task for someone who does not do so with frequency.

Seventy years had elapsed from my first to my second bar mitzvah service. As I prepared my comments, I realized how much more meaning the service would have for me the second time around. I had often questioned whether a boy of 13 has the maturity to appreciate the significance of the traditional "coming of age" ritual. At 83, I could not only reflect on the experience of life, but I could interpret and understand the ritual, the readings, and the process of this second bar mitzvah.

At the conclusion of my second bar mitzvah (in 2006 at age eighty-three), I invite the congregation to join me for my third bar mitzvah at age ninety-six.

The Last of Life for Which the First Was Made

MY DETERMINATION to serve others after having endured the Nazis' attempts to dehumanize me was buoyed by my faith. One cause that captured my attention was benefiting senior citizens. Remembering my own parents as well as the elderly couple in Reichenbach, Germany, who had been willing to risk their own lives to save mine, I became curious about the lives of the elderly. A stint as an officer and board member of a home for the aged had introduced me to the challenges of the aging process and increased my awareness of the special needs of this segment of our population. So I dug in: I observed, learned, and came to appreciate what the home's residents had experienced in their long lives.

Long before I became a senior citizen myself, I served as co-chair of the Senior Legislative Issues Coalition and the Advisory Council on Aging in Union County, New Jersey. As president of the New Jersey State Association of Jewish Federations, an umbrella organization for Jewish philanthropies, I advocated for funding and legislative support for seniors in need of housing and services.

Through this work, I met many seniors who reminded me of this passage in poet Robert Browning's "Rabbi ben Ezra":

Grow old along with me!
The best is yet to be;
The last of life, for which the first was made...

In the United States, generations earlier, 65 had become recognized as the magic age of retirement, followed by the "golden years." Many seniors who could afford to give up working folded up their tents and took their lives in a different direction. They had worked many years and had earned the right to freedom. But freedom from what?

In the process of giving up careers and livelihoods, many—even today—also lose the desire to create and develop, and the drive to seek new challenges. I and my colleague Seymour Epstein, head of a small department store chain, both felt that seniors were capable of undertaking meaningful activities that would sustain them for the last decades of their lives. Toward this end, we raised the capital needed to create a non-profit organization known as Retirement to Renewal: The Center for Change. Its purpose was to reach residents in New Jersey senior housing centers and show them how to retain and use their talents, abilities, and know-how. In the process, we restored their pride and self-esteem.

The program was activity-centered: no lectures, but a lot of leading questions and memory restorers. Participants, reaching back to their earlier productive years, plotted on large charts the activities and abilities they had given up simply because it was "time to retire." My job was to lay out reference points that stimulated their memories of activities that had once been central to their lives. On wall charts the seniors plotted new "career paths" based on their earlier activities.

After a period of reflection, many participants resumed careers or developed new interests that kept them engaged in their communities. Some resumed cooking favorite dishes; others reactivated talents and interests in piano, voice, reading, and even athletics.

The most dramatic transformation I witnessed came from a Holocaust survivor living in a senior housing facility in Cranford, New Jersey. Although she retained memories of the atrocities she had experienced, she had never shared her painful story outside her family. During our sessions together, she found the strength to talk about the events she had buried long before. Telling her story brought her enormous relief and led her to recognize that she had a valuable message for others.

More and more survivors who had similar experiences also began to reveal their Holocaust stories, joining the effort to make sure the world would "never forget."

Some months after the woman in Cranford completed our program, I received a letter from her telling me that she had begun speaking to appreciative audiences at the local YMCA and other community organizations. The responses she was receiving, she wrote, had restored purpose to her life—and her experience was a definite inspiration to me as well, helping me decide to share my own story and to write this book.

Charlie the Bully:
The Young Respond

I THINK I ALWAYS had the urge to lead, but never the conviction. I recall only once exercising my assertiveness (bolstered with a lot of nerve), at Ivy Street Junior High School in Newark. Charlie was a bully who had challenged me to a fight. Word spread through the school that Charlie and I would battle it out when school let out at 3 PM. Crowds of students gathered in the schoolyard. Charlie emerged first, to the applause of many students. When I followed, a few cheered. Charlie was taller, heavier, and looked tough. Somehow, I mustered the courage to defend myself. I thought my athleticism and the belief that I was standing up for what was right would prevail.

Then a strange thing happened. With the crowd waiting in anticipation, Charlie looked at me and said, "Bob, what are we fighting for?"

"I don't know, Charlie," I responded.

He extended his hand, which I shook.

The students, bewildered at first, started to clap and cheer. I was stunned by their reaction. Goodness had prevailed. It was a lesson I never forgot, and which served a purpose years later.

As a survivor of Nazi atrocities, I have spoken to thousands of students on behalf of the Holocaust Council of

Greater MetroWest NJ. One day, on the way to speak at a middle school, the chair of the Holocaust Council, Barbara Wind, asked that I do an additional presentation to students in kindergarten and the first grade.

A little bewildered, I wondered what I might say to children too young to understand the implications of the Holocaust or relate to my wartime experiences as a slave laborer. My inspiration came as we approached the school. At the time, New Jersey and its schools were wrestling with a surge of bullying and were making efforts to deal with the issue. In my remarks to the very young students, I described the bullying incident I had experienced many years ago and how Charlie and I had resolved it peacefully. But then I issued a warning to which these youngsters could relate. I challenged them to learn how to recognize bullying and how to resist bullies. I told them that bullying that got out of hand could lead to extreme cases like Adolf Hitler (the ultimate bully) and the rise of the Nazis, and the loss of many lives.

They understood, and I was rewarded with the satisfaction that I found an appropriate response to a pressured situation.

Preparing the Stage for Volunteer Service

DURING MY LENGTHY hospitalization, the scars inflicted by military service aroused in me the conviction that there must have been a reason for my survival: that I should work to benefit others.

As I received my discharge from the Army in December 1945, my immediate agenda was typical: complete my college education, get a job, get married, and raise a family. That all happened, but my agenda broadened.

After Shirley and I married, we rented the top floor of a tenement building in the Weequahic section of Newark, and later moved to a garden apartment in nearby Orange. One day I received a phone call from a solicitor asking me to contribute to the United Jewish Appeal. I learned that funds raised by UJA were directed to human service organizations, mostly Jewish, but some that served the needs of the general public. Something clicked, and it wasn't the phone.

The tugs on my conscience that I had felt during my hospitalization surfaced. "Who runs the United Jewish Appeal? What does it do?" I asked. Later, the local campaign director briefed me, and I studied the organization's literature. Impressed by the benefits it brought to so many people, I knew I had found a solution to the lingering desire to make my survival, my life, have meaning. It was the beginning of more than 60 years of continuous volunteer service. The organizations I served reflected the diversity of the human needs fulfilled: New Jersey State Association of Jewish Federations, Jewish Federation of Greater MetroWest NJ, Jewish Historical Society of New Jersey, State of Israel Bonds, United Way of Union County, Daughters of Israel Geriatric Center, New Jersey-Israel Commission, Union County Advisory Council on Aging, and the Senior Legislative Issues Coalition. What surprised me was that I developed an appetite for leadership, and took senior positions with most of the organizations, a role in contrast to my wartime and pre-war experiences, when I had never wanted to lead.

As president of the New Jersey State Association of Jewish Federations, I met Governor James Florio of New Jersey at frequent economic development conferences.

*I met frequently with New Jersey Governor Tom Kean and
reviewed services provided by statewide social service agencies.*

*Greeting New Jersey senator and basketball legend
Bill Bradley at a United Jewish Appeal rally.*

CHAPTER 6:
REFLECTION

Reflection

NOW THAT I AM in my 90s, I realize how much my time in the military influenced my post-war life. My first successful business, following years of employment with several companies, was built on an ability to adapt on the spot, to alter tactics and respond more directly to my prospects' needs. That kind of adaptation had often occurred on the battlefield, and it was good training.

In the Army, I also learned a lot about how one's mind and body adjust to the conditions surrounding them. Military life and slave labor taught me how to deal with pain and tolerate emotional highs and lows, hopes, and fears.

I returned to civilian life more disciplined, and I could see how certain experiences had honed that self-control. During my second day in combat, my rifle was blown out of my hands by enemy artillery and I hadn't dug a foxhole for protection. After that, I never again balked at following recommended or required battlefield behavior. I had learned that discipline was essential to staying alive, and this mindset remained with me after the war.

Survivors' Guilt: It Is All About Memory

"IT'S A MIRACLE you remained alive."

I hear this frequently when I speak to adult audiences. On the drive home from speaking engagements, I often reflect on that observation. Yes, many miracles saved me, and it was conscience that converted those miracles to the desire to serve others and meet human needs for the rest of my life.

My roommate in college, Paul Stark, used to tell me that I had a compulsion complex. I think he meant that I was not always content to leave things as they were. If there were a better way to accomplish something, I'd try to find it. I did that as president of both my college fraternity and the campus Hillel organization, shortly after my return to civilian life.

My World War II experiences changed my mindset in many ways. Because I survived, I came to feel that if I wasn't doing all I possibly could, I was cheating. How did I discover my capabilities? Simply by trying. Paul was right; though it took me some time to recognize this, I was incapable of leaving things as they were.

Fifty-five years after I left the Army, I tried on my Army uniform, the one I wore when I was discharged in December 1945. It no longer fit. The jacket with the medals I had earned in combat was scheduled for display at a Holocaust remembrance observance. I was no longer the college kid who had turned down the chance to play saxophone and clarinet in the Army so that he could experience the "real war." My destiny had led me to make a choice that led to a life I never could have predicted.

Since that time, I have followed my heart in an attempt to make sense of the senseless brutality I experienced. I have tried my best to build a life that will give meaning and purpose to my surviving what so many thousands of others did not. I was blessed to have the support, the guidance, and the inspiration of my wife Shirley, who was a community leader in her own right.

In Viktor Frankl's *Man's Search for Meaning* (1946), I found clarification for the urge that first formed during my sleepless nights of hospitalization during and after the war. Frankl, a psychotherapist and Auschwitz survivor, explained that the meaning of life "is to help others find the meaning of theirs." This has become my mission in writing this book; I hope that these pages will finally fulfill that moving search for meaning that occupied the quiet, lonely hours I spent lying awake in a hospital bed, and that my story will resonate with readers who are undertaking quests of their own.

Although my experiences as a slave laborer were painful, unimaginable even, I do not want to go back and erase those days. As Elie Wiesel wrote, "For in the end, it is all about memory, its sources and its magnitude, and, of course, its consequences."

"I Will Never Forget"

I HAVE RECEIVED many letters from students—and teachers and school administrators—who heard my story. Here are some excerpts:

> On behalf of Temple B'nai Abraham Religious School,
> I wish to thank you for sharing your personal story
> with our students. Their Holocaust curriculum is
> brought to life by having you speak about your real-
> life experiences. I know that each of the students has a
> deeper understanding of what it was like to live as Jews
> during that period of time. Many of our classes have
> gone on to study others' stories in depth. It has renewed
> the children's sense of why Jewish commitment and
> community are so important.
>
> What a valuable service you provide for our people and
> our future.
>
> —AN EDUCATOR
>
> I hope this letter can serve as my own appreciation,
> although few words can capture the enrichment I gain
> from my times at the Survivors Speak program.
>
> —AN EDUCATOR
>
> I am lucky because we are probably the last generation
> to hear how life was during the Holocaust by a real
> Holocaust survivor. Again, thank you so much for

coming and telling us about your life. I will never forget it. I will pass it down to my children and others. I hope this will never happen again!

— LAUREN

I truly appreciated your presentation with all my heart. Thanks to you, I learned a sundry of things about the Holocaust and slave labor. The way you explained your experiences was so vivid that it was almost like I had been there too.

Now I truly know what a horrific experience it was to be a slave laborer.

— ISABEL

Your story was extremely powerful and thought-provoking. Your overall message and advice you gave really resonated with me. I can guarantee you that I will honor my pledge to you, and will never let your story vanish.

— ANNA

The Holocaust was a bad period in time. I will not forget it and will pass my experience with you to other children.

— BRADLEY

Now that you have told us your story about being a POW and having no freedom whatsoever, the word "Freedom" means a lot more to me. Every day people take their freedom for granted and never realize what people had to do to get it for them.

— CHLOE

*"Tolerance is the most important thing," and boy did
you have more than just tolerance, you had self-dignity
and the ability to persevere. Freedom is not something
that you can achieve overnight; it is something that is
earned over a period of time. We now have the power to
say that we live in "the land of the free and the home of
the brave."*

— KAYLA

*I was so amazed with your story. I was in awe — that
was really amazing that you survived. Wow! I will
never forget your story as long as I live.*

— SAMANTHA

*You taught me to be courageous. Also you taught me
to never give up and always push harder and someday
something good will come along.*

— RICKY

*Learning about Bob Max's struggle during the
Holocaust has been an experience we will never forget.
We have heard the story of a true American and Jewish
hero. It is a story that will live on for generations, and
we will be there to ensure that this story will never be
forgotten along with the horror of the Holocaust.*

— MICHAEL, SAMMY, MICHAEL, MATT

One Survivor: Student Reactions

"Hearing a real <u>survivor</u> was life changing."

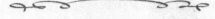

Robert "Bob" Max

"I truly enjoyed listening to Bob's <u>life</u> story."

"HIS COURAGE IS AN <u>INSPIRATION</u> TO THE WORLD."

"My grandfather was a POW during the Korean War. He passed away a few years ago, and he didn't talk about his experience much. When Bob was telling his story, I felt a <u>connection</u> with my grandfather and I am so grateful for that."

"His firsthand account helps you <u>understand</u> the truth of life back then."

"I was so <u>intrigued</u> by his story; I went home to tell my parents about it."

"Hearing Holocaust stories like his
has changed my <u>perspective</u> on my own life for the better."

"I promise to <u>tell</u> your story."

"Thank you so much for <u>sharing</u> your stories!"

**-From Mr. Vito's students
Holocaust/Genocide Studies
Cranford High School**

*Students at Cranford High School in New Jersey
wanted to make sure I got their message.*

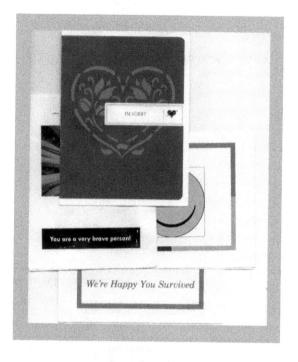

*Students at a high school in New Jersey pooled their
reactions in a package of "love" letters.*

ACKNOWLEDGMENTS

I am deeply grateful to the friends, family, and associates who helped, encouraged, and guided me in writing *The Long March Home*.

Inspired by a weekend Shirley and I spent with Elie Wiesel in 1988, I broke my 53-year silence and started to talk—and later write—about combat, captivity, and escape from slave labor in Nazi Germany during World War II.

Shirley and I meet up again with Elie Wiesel during his visit to the Jewish Federation of Greater Metrowest, New Jersey.

Editors Heidi von Schreiner, Liz Crystal, and Stephanie Kromash Baum helped shape the narrative and make it a "good read." Others inspired and encouraged me to tell my story and its dramatic and sometimes humorous episodes and adventures. Some urged me to write about the influence of the war on the following 60 years of my life, in which I helped others find "meaning in their lives" (Viktor Frankl, *Man's Search for Meaning*).

I greatly appreciate the professional guidance of Linda Forgosh, executive director of the Jewish Historical Society of New Jersey, who helped me meet the standards for the composition of this memoir. I am also grateful to Barbara Wind, director of the Holocaust Council of Greater MetroWest NJ, and to Robert Wiener, Mali Schwartz, David Lippman, Howard Kiesel, and Mark DiIonno, whose writings provided a constructive influence and encouragement.

For inspiring me to write and preserve this story, I thank my daughter, Dr. Wendy Max, and her husband, Dr. Bob Siegel; my son, Doug Max; and my grandchildren, Tayson, Kyler, and Zarek Siegel, and Xander and Emerson Max.

I am grateful to Dov Ben-Shimon, CEO of the Jewish Federation of Greater MetroWest, NJ for his encouragement and recognition of the uniqueness of this story.

ABOUT THE AUTHOR

A lifetime resident of New Jersey, Bob Max served in World War II, enlisting on October 26, 1942. During the Battle of the Bulge on January 4, 1945, he was captured behind German lines, forced into slave labor, and subjected to harsh treatment and starvation. He led a daring escape, reached Allied lines, and was subsequently hospitalized for ten months with more than 20 illnesses and injuries.

He was awarded the Purple Heart with Oak Leaf Cluster, three Bronze Campaign Battle Stars, and the New Jersey Distinguished Service Medal.

In civilian life, he served as president of the New Jersey State Association of Jewish Federations, the Jewish Historical Society of New Jersey, two Jewish congregations, and several businesses; served as the Associate General Chair of Metropolitan NJ State of Israel Bonds; and chaired the Union County Advisory Council on Aging and the Senior Legislative Issues Coalition.

He received the Lasting Impressions Award for 60 years of leadership in the Jewish community and a lobby dedication as a founder with his wife, Shirley, of Congregation Beth Hatikvah in Summit, New Jersey. Endowments in their names were established at Ohio University and Drew University.

Bob Max's life story was recorded and is preserved in the United States Holocaust Memorial Museum in Washington, DC, and the National World War II Museum in New Orleans.